MIRACLE MAN

Judy Landrieu Klein

Praise for *Miracle Man*

"I loved this story: as a human, as a Catholic. You're a wonderful writer... Bernie comes beautifully, vividly alive."

Heather King, Editor of *Miracle Man,* Author and contributor to *Magnificat* monthly prayer book

*****

"This book is a story of a shaking that actually made faith stronger and brought people together. That's the miracle of it all. And the first time I read it, it brought me closer to my God, my wife and my family. It gave me a deeper appreciation of the gift of life, the gift of love, and most especially the gift of faith. Honestly, I think this book will do much the same thing for just about anyone who begins to read it. Begins to read it— because there is no doubt in my mind that anyone who picks up will be unable to put it down."

Marcellino D'Ambrosio, PhD, "Dr. Italy"
Best-selling author and Blogger, Crossroads Initiative

*****

"I had to do violence to myself to put it down...Loved it! I was profoundly moved...I could not read it without frequently sighing, 'Thank you, Lord!' *Miracle Man* is a gift to all of us."

Jimmy Seghers, Biblical Scholar and Theologian
Totus Tuus Ministries

*****

"Whether your soul is over flowing with faith or you find yourself questioning God and asking: 'Why me, God?', Miracle Man is a must read. You'll be left dizzy from the roller-coaster-ride-life of the Klein family. With each page you think, "Surely it can't get any worse." Yet each time, the calamity of events, circumstances and burdens increases. God's presence, in unlikely places, makes Miracle Man a rewarding gift to read."

Gerard Braud, Crisis Communications Expert

"The story…is remarkable and extraordinary…It is a story of fortitude, patience, endurance, and perseverance in our human capacity to love. The love Jesus wants us to put first but the love we often times let "life" put to the side. It is a story of the magnificence of God's amazing grace and His will."

Jane Harvey, Author, *Ask Him* Books

*****

"Such a powerful story of redemption and hope. I could not stop reading it."

Sue Zaunbrecher, *Magnificat Women's Breakfast* Service Team Member, *Lord Teach Me to Pray* Group Facilitator

*****

Wow!…Moved to tears of healing by the story and the great blessing of having shared a portion of the journey as it evolved. Thank you for passing on the mysteries of grace so well.

Fr. Robert Cavalier, Pastor

*****

"*Miracle Man* is a powerful, moving, and very real testament to the Way of the Cross incarnating in the midst of a complex and messy modern life…It is Raw Grief transformed by Almighty God into Raw Grace."

Melanie Arnold
T.O.Carm, M.A. Theology

*****

"This is a beautiful, inspiring story that illustrates God's divine mercy and His saving grace. Highly recommend!"

Ellen Gable Hrkach, Bestselling author of "Stealing Jenny"

Miracle Man

Published and Printed by Dickinson Press/DPZ Technology, LLC
Grand Rapids, MI
United States of America

Cover design by Sue Zaunbrecher

ISBN: 978-1-939909-18-3

This book is available at: www.memorareministries.com

www.dpztechnology.com

Dedication

To my five precious children - Kara, Alexandra, Gabrielle, Christian and Benjamin. Your lives have been an immeasurable gift and you have taught me countless rich and rewarding lessons of the heart. I love each of you more than words could ever say.

Table of Contents

"For this reason I kneel before the Father,
from whom every family in heaven and on earth is named,
that he may grant you in accord with the riches of his glory to be
strengthened with power through his Spirit in the inner self,
and that Christ may dwell in your hearts through faith;
that you, rooted and grounded in love,
may have strength to comprehend with all the holy ones
what is the breadth and length and height and depth,
and to know the love of Christ that surpasses knowledge,
so that you may be filled with all the fullness of God.

Now to him who is able to accomplish far more than all we ask or
imagine,
by the power at work within us,
to him be glory in the church and in Christ Jesus to all generations,
forever and ever. Amen."

Ephesians 3:14-21

Foreword

We live in a society that, if it believes in God at all, believes in a deity who is remote, far from the real struggles that we grapple with each day. Our lives consist of challenge after challenge, it seems. But there is no greater crisis than to find oneself suddenly on the brink of the grave. To stare death in the face is to be shaken to the depths of one's being. To linger at death's threshold for days, weeks, and months often shakes faith and families completely apart.

This book is a story of a shaking that actually made faith stronger and brought people together. That's the miracle of it all. And the first time I read it, it brought me closer to my God, my wife and my family. It gave me a deeper appreciation of the gift of life, the gift of love, and most especially the gift of faith. Honestly, I think this book will do much the same thing for just about anyone who begins to read it. Begins to read it— because there is no doubt in my mind that anyone who picks up will be unable to put it down.

Yes, it is a riveting story full of both agony and ecstasy, tears and profound joy. This is the kind of drama that makes for a best selling novel. But this book is not fiction. It's real life. And it's unsanitized and unwhitewashed, with everyone's rough edges left exposed for the reader to see. That's what makes this book so relatable.

The ability of the actors in this drama to laugh in the midst of crisis challenges us to stop and recognize the humor in the midst of our own drama. And even more important than helping us find humor amidst it all, maybe it will help us recognize God amidst it all.

Marcellino D'Ambrosio ("Dr. Italy")

Prologue

People say you die the way you lived. That was surely the case with my husband Bernie, who took us on the ride of our lives during the three months he spent in the ICU following a massive heart attack the day before Christmas Eve, 2008. Bernie lived his life with high drama and intense passion. Those were the qualities that initially attracted me to him —and they were the same qualities that would keep me holding on to the edge of my seat during our twenty-four years of marriage, driving me at times to the brink of insanity. Bernie died with equal drama and passion— so much so, that he earned the name "Miracle Man" among the medical staff that cared for him in the Cardiac Intensive Care Unit.

This is the story of Bernie's journey into the miraculous realm amid a critical illness that would tear the veil between heaven and earth, allowing us a glimpse of heaven *on* earth. It is the story of the "Miracle Man," the name the doctors and nurses affectionately began to call Bernie because he "died and resurrected" so many times, it was clear that something otherworldly was happening to him.

This is Bernie's story, and it is my story. It is also everyone's story, as I believe we are all meant to experience the glory of God as it pierces the natural realm, often in the most unlikely ways and places— such as when it imprints itself visibly in our bodies or invisibly transforms our hearts, like it did with Bernie and me. Moreover, we are not only meant to witness God's glory, we are created to *bear* God's glory. But that is only possible if we are capable of bearing its great weight. And the piercing glory of God can sometimes make for seemingly unbearable weight, as Bernie and I discovered time and time again.

I have come to understand that our capacity to bear God is directly contingent upon the expansiveness of our openness to the hidden gifts life brings, which often arrive in unexpected packages that we did not order. Although our openness is in many cases expanded by the wonderful, joyful surprises of life, it is never so fully stretched as in the midst of the great surprise of suffering. Suffering is, in fact, the great dilator of our capacity for God, precisely because it challenges our notions of Him so profoundly. It forces us to give birth to new ways of thinking about God, and in the end, it will either open us up more deeply to His penetrating love or it will prompt us to close ourselves off to it entirely. That closing ourselves off is hell.

This is a story about opening. Opening to new possibilities about who God is and about who we are called to be. Opening to the honesty of the messiness of our journey into salvation, which has never been a neat, clean event. And opening to the powerful lessons of love, which in the final analysis, are what this journey is meant to teach us.

In truth, I was tempted to sanitize the story and tell only the good parts, the beautiful parts, the holy parts. There were plenty of those to tell. But that would not be true to Bernie or to me. More importantly, it would not be true to God. God is in the details, and many of the details of our lives are just plain messy. I hope you are not scandalized by this fact. Christ certainly was not. The Crucifixion is forever the biggest scandal of all.

This is a true story—a real love story about an extraordinary journey that would tear the hearts of me and my family apart to test the full extent of human love and the infinitude of God's love, as we stared down death together for eighty-seven long days. I pray that it will bless you, and that you will find the miracle of your own God-story amidst the telling of this very human, yet truly divine, real life tale.

I have changed the names of the medical personnel and some of the priests who cared for Bernie to protect their privacy. Otherwise, I have conveyed the account with as much accuracy and honesty as possible. The "Bernie Updates" are taken verbatim from the e-mails I sent to friends while Bernie was hospitalized.

Judy Landrieu Klein
March 19, 2013
The Feast of St. Joseph

The Calm Before the Storm

December 21, 2008

5:00 p.m.

It's four days before Christmas, and I'm sitting in the front courtyard of our home, which is situated near the end of a cul-de-sac in the idyllic Louisiana neighborhood where my husband Bernie and I have raised our five children. The house is thirty-five miles from New Orleans, the city where I was born and raised among the large Landrieu clan, one of the most prominent family names in Louisiana politics. My Uncle "Moon," my father Joseph's only sibling, was Mayor of New Orleans from 1970-1978, and then Secretary of Housing and Urban Development under the Carter administration. Marrying their college sweethearts just two weeks apart in 1954, the young love birds—my father and Uncle Moon— managed to eke out nineteen children in eleven years between them. A set of twins put my parents, affectionately known as the "J. Landrieus," in the lead with seven boys and three girls. The "M. Landrieus" took a respectable second place with five girls and four boys, three of whom are in politics today, currently serving as the Mayor of New Orleans, a United States Senator and a Court of Appeals judge.

I am the sixth child and baby girl of the "J. Landrieus," and I broke my mother's heart by "moving away" from home not long after Bernie and I married—to a "foreign land" a full forty-five minutes north of the city into the gated community where Bernie and I have spent the past twenty-four years. It's a well-known fact among New Orleanians that leaving home is verboten. But we fled to the safety and security of the suburbs anyway when the crack and crime epidemic hit "the city that care forgot" in the mid-eighties, bringing us to a large, contemporary home on the golf course behind the guarded entrance of "Beau Chene," which is French for "beautiful oak."

We've lived in four houses in Beau Chene since then, buying our current home fourteen years ago despite my verbal protests that it was the "ugliest house I'd ever seen" and against my strenuous objections to living in our fourth modern California-style home in a row. Though I desperately wanted to build an Acadian plantation that reflected Louisiana's culture, Bernie likes contemporary architecture, and since it's his way or the

1

highway, a California contemporary with high ceilings and large glass windows throughout was what we got.

Initially, I was appeased by Bernie's promise of a total renovation. I never dreamed, however, that I'd have to endure six renovations in fourteen years—with the last four occurring during the past thirty-six months—leaving us in a constant state of upheaval inside our home. Those recent make-overs were the result of a drought-related five-inch drop in the back of the house, an overflowing toilet that collapsed the entire kitchen ceiling while we were on vacation, a post-Katrina pine tree that was dropped through the center of the house, *and* a subsequent fire due to damaged electrical wiring. We have jokingly concluded that the house must be situated on an Indian burial ground, as it has been "cursed" with repeated episodes of new destruction every time we get it fixed.

Louisiana is thick with Native American history: the Choctaw and Ouachita Indians both settled in our neighborhood, and there are streets in our subdivision named after each tribe. The last house we owned was on Choctaw Place, and the house before that was on Kiskatom Lane, an Indian word for the hickory trees that peppered the property before the golf course was built. Though we've kidded a lot about the house being cursed, I've sometimes wondered deep down if my family was cursed as well, though I would never dare to speak those words out loud.

The house has served as an interesting metaphor for our lives, as the more frantically we have tried to rebuild it, the more calamity we have seemed to encounter. Every time we've said "surely the worst is over," something more terrible has happened. Nine years ago, my thirty-five-year-old brother Scott committed suicide. Four years ago, Bernie's thirty-six-year-old son Marshall died unexpectedly of sudden and unexplained liver failure. Nine months ago, we lost my second-oldest brother Stephen and his fifty-two-year-old wife Brenda through murder-suicide. This most recent trauma really knocked us to our knees. In addition, by September, our eighteen-year-old son Christian had spiraled completely out of control to drug addiction.

It's December now and we just returned home from Family Week at Christian's drug rehab program in Tennessee. I spent the entire week praying that our nineteen-year-old daughter—whose baby is due this month—would not go into labor while we were gone, since I'm her labor coach. I'm frazzled beyond belief and feel that I'm teetering on the edge of a cliff, trying not to fall off. I keep half-joking that if this weren't my life, I wouldn't believe it. I know I could not have made all of this up.

2

During more serious moments I find myself praying constantly, "Please God, let this be it for now." Mother Teresa once said that humility comes through humiliation, and I'm plenty darn humble by now. I'm a Catholic theologian with a public ministry trying to share the good news of Jesus Christ with others, and I can't stop crying about all of the bad news in my life. I've been teaching courses on Christian marriage for years, and my marriage is at the breaking point from the stress. I've preached to others about the power of prayer, yet I feel like my life is falling apart and I'm impotent to stop it no matter how much I pray. Besides that, I've been in a full-blown crisis of faith since March 12, the day my brother Stephen shot and killed his wife and himself, because I can't wrap my mind around the endless cycle of tragedy and problems in our lives. People are starting to refer to me as Job and I'm beginning to believe it. "What am I doing wrong here, God?" I constantly ask.

My husband Bernie, on the other hand, who's a cross between Jack Nicholson and Robert De Niro with his sarcastic sense of humor and aggressive, bigger-than-life personality—but who's a dead ringer (looks wise) for George on "Seinfeld" with his paunchy belly and bald scalp encircled by a rim of black hair—stands like a boxer with his fists pointed at God. In his typical irreverent manner, which I mostly find hysterically funny, he says "Come on, sucker. Hit me again!"

Bernie is one of the most passionate, creative, intelligent and versatile human beings I have ever known. He's also one of the most arrogant, stubborn and impulsive people I've ever known. Because he gets what he likes to call "easily over-entertained," he's had numerous and varied careers throughout his life including Marine Sergeant, computer programmer, internal auditor, advertising and public relations executive, financial consultant, deal broker and crisis management expert—all of which he's attacked with equal vigor. He's also a self-trained legal specialist when necessity calls for it, which generally occurs when one of his clients must file for bankruptcy to restructure their debt, or when they are forced to appear at a bankruptcy court hearing, whereupon Bernie personally offers counsel to help them to fend off creditors.

People are constantly asking Bernie if he's been to law school, because he draws up legal documents and contracts regularly for business deals. "No," he says, "I could have never been a lawyer, because it involves too much bull crap." But he's learned over time that the legal programs that you buy and install on your own computer can be a beautiful thing. Furthermore, though our children have never been able to figure out exactly what Bernie does for a living, he's learned that the all-encompassing title of "management consultant" is the perfect umbrella term for his many and varied business dealings, whatever they may entail at the moment.

The stress and chaos of the past few years have taken their toll on both of us, and the added pressure of the economic fallout this year, which cost Bernie a major government contract, hasn't helped. Bernie happily scored a state contract four years ago to develop The Maritime Institute for Emergency Monitoring and Response (MIEMAR), which was slated to specialize in training personnel to respond to a maritime disaster impacting the Gulf of Mexico or the mouth of the Mississippi River. The institute was Bernie's brainchild, which he conceptualized and developed the year before Hurricane Katrina hit, after he concluded quite prophetically that Louisiana was totally unprepared to deal with a large-scale catastrophe.

Though Bernie worked diligently on the MIEMAR project for several years, one stroke of a pen during the Governor's line item veto this past June brought the project funding to a screeching halt, along with most of the income we were depending on for the next year. That unforeseen setback severely jolted Bernie's morale and left him totally off balance, scrambling to rebuild his business at the age of sixty-three. Thankfully, he is finally seeing the light by signing several new contracts just this week, including one with the Louisiana Organ Foundation to raise public awareness about the need for organ donation. I'm relieved that we've survived this latest round of crisis, and even more relieved that my husband appears to have disproved his theory that he can't reinvent himself again.

Bernie jokes that he can be whatever people want or need him to be, as long as he lands the deal. "You want me to be a Jew from New York, I'm a Jew from New York," he grins, as he spreads his upward-facing palms in front of himself imitating Marlon Brando's accent in "The Godfather." "You want me to be a Catholic from Colombia, I'm a Catholic from Colombia...Hey, you like it, I like it," he quips as I giggle at him. Bernie is actually a half-German, half-Hispanic immigrant from Bogota, Colombia, whose paternal great-grandmother was a Jewish woman named Emily Stein—a fact about which he is extremely proud.

His father Henry's family emigrated from Germany to Bogota just before Hitler rose to power. Then the whole clan, including Henry's young Colombian wife Leticia and three small children, moved to New Orleans when Bernie was four. Unable to speak a word of English, Bernie learned to use his natural charisma and sense of humor to survive among the nuns

4

at Holy Rosary School in New Orleans, where he and his siblings went to grammar school. Then-Bishop Ott secured scholarships for the three children to attend Holy Rosary after he met Bernie's mother at Mass and learned that they were enrolled in public schools.

To this day, Bernie carries a charming, Holy Rosary-learned, boyish grin on his face, and he's kept me in stitches for years with his satirical, dry sense of humor. One thing we've both learned is that humor is a key ingredient to staying sane, especially when you have as much drama and tragedy in life as we have. I am Bernie's best audience, though our children fail to understand just what it is that I find so funny about him. Our daughter Kara, the eldest of our five children together, who is a Christian singer and chastity speaker, glared at me constantly throughout her surprise sixteenth birthday trip to New York City as I laughed hysterically at Bernie for five straight days. "I fail to see what you think is so funny," she'd say, rolling her eyes as I doubled over at his antics.

Kara finally gained some insight into that mystery on the same trip, when we returned to the hotel exhausted and famished late one afternoon following a long day of sightseeing. We decided to pick up some snacks to hold us over until dinner, and Kara and I wanted Starbucks and fruit.

"You girls don't know anything about eating for energy on a trip!" Bernie smirked in a condescending tone. "Look! A deli!" he said excitedly as he spotted Nathan's New York Deli on the corner near our hotel. "I'll show you girls what kind of food you get in New York to keep your energy up," he boasted as he strutted in. Piling a bag full of Swiss cheese, hard salami, rye bread, and Kosher pickles, Bernie quickly led us back to the hotel and feverishly devoured all of the food in a way that only he could eat. Within minutes, he was passed out on the bed drooling and snoring loudly while we laughed uproariously about the stupid "energy food." We tease him about that story to this day.

Although I am Bernie's biggest fan, I can also be his worst critic, as his strong will, impulsivity and stubbornness in decision-making leave me complaining that he "rides herd over me" all of the time. Furthermore, his hot, Latin temper has provoked many a hurt feeling among family and friends, and he thinks nothing of yelling at people at the drop of a hat, including his clients—then forgetting about it completely five minutes later and asking the offended party if they want to go to lunch! The kids and I, who have been intimidated by Bernie's temper for years, stare in disbelief as he screams at one particular client over the phone regularly.

We find it hard to believe that someone actually pays good money for such a tongue-lashing, but the client keeps coming back. That's because he knows he can count on Bernie's wit and tenacity in solving problems, and on the fact that Bernie absolutely never gives up a fight.

"I was a Marine!" my husband says proudly. "And they taught us to kill the enemy or destroy his will to live!" he says in his military voice as he salutes. Bernie carries a tremendous sense of love and respect for the Marine Corps, because it was there that he became a man and discovered his personal and professional gifts. Though his raging alcoholic father insisted he'd never amount to anything and said he'd probably wind up in jail, Bernie disproved his father when he enlisted in the Marines when he was nineteen years old at the height of the Vietnam War. After floundering as a Freshman at LSU in Baton Rouge and nearly flunking out of college, Bernie spontaneously marched himself into the Marine Corps recruiting office one day and signed up. Within weeks he found himself at Camp Pendleton Marine Base in San Diego, California, and he figured out very quickly that it was do or die.

"The first morning, they played 'Reveille' at five a.m. and the sergeant came into our room screaming at the top of his lungs that it was time for us no-good-so-and-so's to get our behinds out of bed!" Bernie remembers. "It was freezing cold and we had been given only a light wool blanket, and I was shivering in a panic and thinking 'what the hell have I done?' Within a few weeks, someone had committed suicide because the training was so rigorous that they couldn't hack it. They break you down completely and then rebuild you as a Marine!" Bernie explains with dramatic, military-like effect.

Seeing that the choices were sink or swim, Bernie decided to swim—and swim he did! He graduated from his class of cadets with the Honor Man Award, the Leadership Award, the Physical Excellence Award, the Rifleman Award and the Academic Excellence Award. Sadly, no one from his family was able to attend his graduation and share in his accolades, so another family from Louisiana, who felt sorry for him because his parents and siblings weren't present, took him to lunch to celebrate. Bernie still operates like a Marine when it comes to crisis and conflict, and I've seen him win more seemingly impossible battles than I can shake a stick at. After twenty-four years of marriage, I've learned that Bernie will inevitably land on his feet no matter how fast he seems to be free falling during a crisis, because he knows how to survive when he has to. And boy, has he had to.

Bernie and I are complete opposites when it comes to dealing with people and problems, as I tend to be passive and freeze with fear in the midst of crisis. In fact, I often shut down completely. I remind myself regularly that "Bernardo," as he is known in his family, is a Colombian immigrant with a pure German father and a pure Colombian mother while I am a New Orleans bred American woman. I concluded long ago that the differences between us are cultural as much as they are personality driven, and that's not going to change in this lifetime. Besides, the fact that Bernie is fifteen-and-a-half years older than me means that we hail from two different generations, and he still operates under the paradigm that men go to work and make the decisions while women go to church and care for the house and kids. Above all, he believes that a man should be treated as king of the castle at all times when he is home—a lesson that he took from his own parents which he reminds me of with regularity. That reality alone taught me to pray the Serenity Prayer daily—when it became crystal clear to me one night while I exhaustedly washed the dishes after a long day of caring for four young children while Bernardo lounged on the sofa that I had two choices—either accept the things I cannot change or be angry for the rest of my life.

Though there's been plenty of anger in our marriage, there's been lots of love and laughter too. After nearly a quarter of century of married life, I've concluded that marriage, like life, is a mixed bag. And like my mother-in-law Letty has told me a million times in her heavy Columbian accent: "If you want to stay married, you have to put up with a lot!"

December 21, 2008

Suppertime

Basking in the late afternoon sun, I admire the many beautiful flowers and plants that are still in full bloom in our walled brick gardens and terracotta ceramic pots, which are plenteous in the New Orleans style courtyard that graces the front of our home. I'm grateful for the warm Louisiana December and the fact that the flowers I planted in the fall, including a thick cascade of white petunias, somehow survived the highly unusual five inches of snow that blanketed the south just two weeks ago. I look around the courtyard admiringly, thanking God for the serene refuge it has provided during these difficult times. Bernie and I have both enjoyed countless hours of pleasure in the enclosed refuge with its whitewashed brick walls, calming center fountain and beautiful wrought iron fences, which Bernie painstakingly designed himself. Though he gloats constantly about his meticulous planning and execution of the space, which he created and built for me because I wanted a place to pray, it is indeed a slice of heaven on earth and his vision for it was truly inspired.

Never mind the fact that the uninsured tree cutters he hired to clear the land for the construction of the courtyard back on November 1, 2005 dropped a massive pine tree through our house as they prepared the spot where the fountain would go. And forget about the fact that the tree would have killed me as it plummeted through the center of our home had I not listened to an insistent voice in my spirit telling me repeatedly, "Leave the house...leave the house now!!!!" as I watched the men sawing the tree from the living room. Thankfully, after the third or fourth warning, I decided to go stand in the driveway in order to watch in safety while the men dropped the two-ton, seventy-foot tree into the street. No such luck. I stood in utter shock as I heard a loud snap and watched the tree fall like a bomb through our house, landing exactly where I had been standing only minutes before.

My first reaction was to run around in circles in the street like a wild banshee screaming every curse word I could think of at the top of my lungs, jumping up and down like a madwoman with each expletive I shouted. I can still see my neighbor Marcia's face as she watched the surreal scene, and I must admit, she looked a little frightened. But once I got that out of my system, I immediately remembered it was All Saints Day, and that thought brought me strange consolation. "Maybe we're supposed to be in solidarity with the thousands of families who just lost

8

their homes to Katrina," I thought as I stood in the street surveying the damage. The consolation was short-lived as my rage about my husband's recklessness began to mount, especially since he promised to stay home to supervise the men, then left unexpectedly to attend an "emergency" meeting in New Orleans shortly after the tree cutting crew arrived.

I had been extremely grateful to God for sparing our house just two months earlier when Hurricane Katrina hit, even though the water was "lapping at our back door," as my friend Cecil so eloquently put it. Katrina had not only swamped the City of New Orleans with ten feet of water when the levees protecting the city broke on that fateful day in August, but the tidal surge she brought with her swept away miles and miles of houses and buildings along the Mississippi Gulf Coast, leaving the city and the coast looking like a nuclear bomb had been detonated.

As our home is forty-five minutes north of New Orleans and an hour west of the Gulf Coast, the damage to our area was caused primarily from falling pine trees, along with some flooding from the overflowing banks of Tchefuncte River which buttresses the golf course at the end of our cul-de-sac. It was those waters that lapped at our back door during Katrina without entering the house.

"The fact that your house didn't flood is an absolute miracle," Cecil said when we spoke after the hurricane, which she and her husband Johnny decided to "ride out" at home. "We walked behind your house and I swear, if the water had come up a quarter of an inch higher, your house would have flooded."

"It IS a miracle," I told Cecil after hearing her eyewitness report. "I entrusted our home to Our Lady of Prompt Succor as we walked out of the door and apparently she interceded to save it." That belief was confirmed when we returned home from evacuating to Memphis to find that pine trees had fallen in a perfect square around the house, with some of them just inches from the structure. But none had hit the house, thanks to Our Lady.

Our Lady of Prompt Succor, one of the myriad of names for the Virgin Mary and which means "quick help" in French, is the Patron Saint of the City of New Orleans because she has saved the city from fire, war, plagues, and hurricanes in the past. Though Louisiana is part of the Bible belt, New Orleans is a profoundly Catholic city, and every Catholic Church in the Archdiocese of New Orleans prays for Our Lady of Prompt Succor's intercession at the end of Mass throughout hurricane season.

Over the years, we have seen numerous hurricanes heading straight for New Orleans change their path at the last minute, and Katrina was no exception. I like to remind people that Our Lady had, in fact, saved New Orleans from Hurricane Katrina, as the hurricane didn't directly hit the city. But she hadn't been able to save New Orleans from the Corps of Engineers, who'd failed to maintain the levees around the city, leading to the catastrophic post-Katrina flood. And she hadn't been able to save our home from Bernie who, against my vigorous protests, had hired an uninsured, inexperienced "friend of a friend" to cut down a massive pine tree that stood only feet from the house—a project that not only requires great expertise and precision, but INSURANCE in case the tree-cutter screws up.

After my street dance, I'd gathered my nerve to approach the tree-cutter, who was sitting on the ground in a daze staring into space.

"What the hell happened?" I asked him incredulously. All he could say in his thick southern drawl as he sat shamefaced on the edge of the street was, "I stood there for hours trying to decide if I should cut that tree down. But I really wanted to impress Mr. Bernie. Now I've impressed him the wrong way!"

"Yeah, you idiot, this IS impressive," I thought to myself as I stood looking at our roofless house with a two-ton pine tree lying through the middle of it, noting how the tree had peeled the roof off the house as it fell, much like one peels back a can of sardines.

"How are we going to live in a house without a roof?" I asked. "Sweet Jesus, I pray it doesn't rain."

We hadn't had a drop of rain since Katrina hit on August 29, two months earlier. That was a miracle in and of itself, due to the fact that so many homes were without roofs after the hurricane and rain would have only added insult to the already grievous injury. The tree slammed through the house on November 1st, and since we had no roof, I prayed that the drought would continue. As I stood in the street worrying about rain, a man I'd never seen before raced up in a truck to say that he'd heard what sounded like a bomb exploding several blocks away where he was working and had come to see what happened. Without a word of warning, he started pulling equipment out of his truck and proceeded to install a plastic "Blue Roof" on our house—a blue, vinyl tarp which had become the standard, temporary emergency roof in Louisiana since Katrina. When he finished, he'd shaken my hand, jumped into his truck and left without another word. I have no idea who that man was to this day, but I do know that we got record rainfall that very night. Had that unknown angel not shown up that afternoon with an unordered Blue Roof, the interior of our home and our belongings would have been completely ruined as well, including the extensive art collection Bernie had accumulated over thirty years. God does work in mysterious ways.

A short time later, Bernie finally arrived home to survey the damage and the first words out of his mouth, incredibly, were, "Give me a check to pay the man."

"What????" I asked in disbelief.

"Give me a check," he reiterated. "I have to pay the man."

"We are not paying that man!" I shot back angrily. "He just destroyed our home!!!"

"Judy, give me a check right now!" Bernie demanded in a stern voice. "The poor man spent a lot of money renting that equipment and I am going to reimburse him for it."

Yep, that was Bernie. I never knew what he was going to do or what to expect, and living with him was like living on a roller-coaster ride. The pine-tree-through-the-roof was just one of many such incidents that have occurred during our marriage, leaving me simmering with anger for weeks or even months until some normalcy returned to our lives or until the next crisis was created. Though the house took an entire year and a whopping $200,000 to rebuild, three years later we now both absolutely love the place with its stucco exterior and attached courtyard. I try to forget about the insanity that precipitated the makeover because it just makes me angry all over again. And, as Bernie says, "So what if there was a little mishap along the way? It turned out beautifully in the end."

Well, yes and no. Though the house does finally have a touch of the Louisiana architectural feel that I wanted in the first place, I could have done without the trauma to get it a full frontal facelift. I still vividly remember feeling like I was falling off a cliff and waking with a startled gasp every time I dozed off for weeks after the near-miss with death, as well as my recurring nightmare of trying to run from the falling tree. I cringe to this day wondering what would have happened if I hadn't obeyed the voice and left the house, knowing full well I would have probably been crushed, as I've never been fast on my feet. I try not to let myself think

11

about that either. That was life with Bernie: the highs, the lows; the Cross, the Resurrection, all rolled into one.

As I stare at the petunias, hibiscuses and geraniums on display in their ceramic pots, my mind instantly wanders to all the other tasks that need to be done to get ready for Christmas. The dirt bike has to be assembled for our youngest son Benjamin, who is nine. I have to get some last minute shopping done for our three daughters—Kara, twenty-two, Alex, twenty-one, and Gaby, nineteen—and for James Gabriel, the baby whom Gaby has already named and who is due in a week. And I need to stop at Baby 'N Me tomorrow to pick up the blue letters that spell James' name so we can finish the nursery. I already mailed a guitar to Christian, who is eighteen and will be spending Christmas at the in-patient rehab program in Tennessee. With a wave of anxiety, I realize there's plenty more to do before Christmas arrives in four short days.

As I and the rest of the family go about our business, none of us can know that within forty-eight short hours our lives will be blown apart with more violence than we could have dreamed possible. And none of us can know what we will have to endure before everything "turns out beautifully in the end."

Going Places

Bernie and I met through a mutual friend who had worked with each of us separately at the Louisiana World Exposition, or "World's Fair," that was held in New Orleans in 1984. Bernie was coming off of a divorce to his first wife Marsha after sixteen years of marriage and two children, when he decided to leave a high-paying job as Manager of Internal Auditing at a large oil company in Dallas to become an entrepreneur and put on trade shows at the World's Fair.

Within a short time, Bernie had gained so much notoriety for his trade shows and for the publicity that he generated around them that a local businessman suggested he start a public relations agency—which he promptly did—with the same businessman's company as his first client—despite the fact that Bernie knew nothing about the public relations industry. The only two jobs he'd had since the Marines were working as a computer programmer for the City of Los Angeles for fifteen years, and then as an oil company executive in Dallas for three, but that didn't stop Bernie from diving headlong into the public relations and advertising business, or from winning numerous awards over the years for the phenomenally creative campaigns he conceptualized and developed. His clients would eventually include the New Orleans City Ballet, the New Orleans Symphony Orchestra, the New Orleans Opera Association and the New Orleans Museum of Art—quite fitting since Bernie held a B.A. in Art History from Pepperdine University in California and absolutely loved the arts.

For my part, I had graduated from Loyola University in New Orleans in 1982 with a B.A. in Communications and gone straight from college to work on former Governor Edwin Edwards' re-election campaign staff, where he would win an historic bid for a third term as governor of Louisiana. The bumper stickers that read "Re-elect the Crook" should have sent me scurrying in the opposite direction, but given that I was never a great judge of character and always tended to be attracted to people who lived on the edge, I ran headlong into the political arena, thinking it would be familiar terrain after having been around politics all my life. I spent six months opening and managing Edwards' headquarters in New Orleans before moving to the central campaign office in the state capital of Baton Rouge for a year. While stationed there, I traveled around the state by private plane and helicopter several nights a week with Edwards' brother Marion putting on rallies in various cities throughout Louisiana.

My experience in the successful Edwards campaign had its strong points, but being totally naïve, I expected to find there a family-run campaign much like the ones I knew as a child. During numerous elections throughout our lives, my Aunt Verna Landrieu and mother Phyllis brought all nineteen of us children to work as volunteers at campaign headquarters —answering phones, licking and sticking envelopes, applying postage stamps and doing anything and everything that a given political campaign demanded. In contrast, what I found in the Edwards operation was an environment for adults only, and though I was by no means a prude, I was scandalized by the sexual permissiveness and free-flowing immorality that I witnessed in the Edwards camp. For instance, before winning the election Edwards, who was still married to his first wife Elaine, famously quipped to reporters: "The only way I can lose this election is if I'm caught in bed with either a dead girl or a live boy." That statement summed up in one sentence the attitudinal environment I experienced working in his campaign.

When the campaign ended in late 1983, I was deeply depressed over the debauchery I had witnessed and the relationships I had formed during my time there. One relationship that affected me deeply was a close friendship with a woman named Lola—the mistress of a prominent businessman who was arrested for murdering his wife just weeks after the election was over. Though the man claimed his wife had committed suicide and was eventually acquitted of the crime, he had been detained by police and posted bail the day before he invited Lola and me to come for dinner at his mansion. I was extremely hesitant to accept the invitation, but agreed to go after Lola insisted that her friend could really use some company after his arrest and expensive bailout the day before.

We arrived at his home around seven p.m., whereupon the businessman immediately offered to give me a tour of the place. He then proceeded to walk me through his wife's bedroom, where bloody sheets still lay on the bed and police tape marked off the crime scene, to an adjoining bedroom to show me where the police had found the gun she allegedly killed herself with hidden under a pillow. By the time we got to the attic wine cellar my knees were literally knocking, and I was genuinely convinced that he was going to kill me because he thought I knew too much. Instead, he concluded the tour in the dining room where Lola was waiting for us. I hastily forced some dinner down my throat before bowing out gracefully, trying not to make it obvious that I was terrified.

Shaken to the core by that event, I decided to get as far away from politics as possible. I left Baton Rouge immediately and returned to New

Orleans to job hunt, turning down the Governor's personal offer to work in his administration. The move back home would soon lead me to the World's Fair, and ultimately to Klein and Associates Public Relations a year later.

Quite ironically, it is Edwin Edwards whom I credit with causing my adult Christian conversion, which occurred on the heels of his election. Though I had been raised as a Catholic, I had lost my faith in God at a Catholic college. After being presented with a deconstructed and relativistic version of "truth" in the many theology and philosophy classes I took there, I graduated from college as an agnostic moving toward atheism. My stint in the Edwards campaign and the events surrounding it left me leaning heavily toward the sorry conclusion that God must indeed be dead. At the same time, however, I was fervently begging God to show me once and for all if He existed. It was in the midst of that beseeching that I was unexpectedly invited by my cousin's cousin to attend a Protestant church service on Tulane University's campus, and I hesitantly agreed to go. At the end of his sermon, the pastor asked the congregation if we wanted to know if God was real, and that He had a plan for our lives. He invited us to pray "The Sinner's Prayer," whereupon he led us in prayer to acknowledge our sinfulness and our need for a Savior. With every ounce of yearning and despair that was smoldering inside me, I gave my heart and my life to Jesus Christ that day, hoping against hope that He would show up for me.

Bells didn't ring and fireworks did not go off, but in one instant I went from not knowing if God existed to knowing beyond a shadow of a doubt that God was real, that He knew and loved me personally, and that I was called to enter into a living relationship with Him. It was a St. Paul-type conversion experience that dramatically changed my life, and my entire world went from heavy darkness to warm light in one split second. That was twenty-four years ago and I have never questioned God's existence for a moment since that day, even though I've shaken my fist at Him more than a few times in the midst of the multiplicity of suffering life has presented.

Just weeks after my conversion experience, I landed a job as the Talent Relations Supervisor in the Amphitheatre at the 1984 New Orleans World's Fair—a job that would put me in charge of airport transit and backstage accommodations for the numerous stars who came to perform at the Fair, including Bob Hope, Andy Williams and Julio Iglesias, along with popular bands like the Bee Gees and The Go Go's. My most vivid World's Fair memory is the night music legend Cab Calloway refused to

15

perform because, not grasping the full extent of his renown, I put him in a dressing room with the band of newly famous jazz artist Wynton Marsalis, while giving Wynton his own dressing room. After using a string of peppery words to communicate his displeasure, Calloway jumped into the back of a cab and sped off to the airport, ignoring my pleading apologies for him to stay and perform in the show. I learned that day that ignorance is not necessarily bliss and I was plenty embarrassed by the snafu, even though my bosses at the Fair went fairly easy on me.

When the World's Fair ended, my friend Deena, who was in charge of organizing the Fair's trade shows, called to tell me that I "had to" get on board with Klein and Associates Public Relations right away. "Bernie Klein is one of the most brilliant men I have ever met," she told me "and he is going places." I phoned Bernie that afternoon to inquire about a job, and after we talked on the phone for an hour about everything under the sun, I hung up and thought to myself, "I'm going to marry that man." I had the same hunch at the job interview with him days later on October 30, 1984, in spite of the fact that I had been seriously dating a Loyola law student for four years. Needless to say, that relationship came to a screeching halt and within six months, after an electric time of working together and a whirlwind romance, Bernie and I were married by the Protestant pastor from the church where I had received Christ. I was twenty-four and Bernie was forty.

Though the pastor was none too happy when he learned that I was pregnant, I was madly in love with Bernie and wanted nothing more than to marry him. I loved his strong, bigger than life personality, his incredible enthusiasm and over the top confidence. Having been a middle child and people-pleasing peacemaker in my own family of ten children with very little identity of my own—and a very insecure person who obsessed over what others thought of me—I appreciated Bernie's strong identity, forthrightness in speaking his mind, and the fact that he didn't give a hoot whom he offended or what others thought of him. Being a fearful person, I admired the fearlessness with which Bernie lived his life and the way that he went after anything he wanted, including me. I could see that he was indeed going places at lightning speed, and I wanted him to take me along for the ride. Besides that, I was convinced that I would be instrumental in saving his soul, and I had already started bringing him to church with me in the hopes he, too, would give his life to Christ.

All of that probably equaled a classic case of co-dependency and a recipe for serious marital conflict when the enthrallment of being opposites waned, but no one could have convinced me of that then, even though some friends and family tried. One naysayer was Bernie's younger sister Hedy, who took me to lunch after she learned Bernie and I were engaged. Being a very devout Catholic, she had heard that I was a born-again Christian and figured she could talk some sense into me.

"Honey," she began in her unabashed manner as I looked into her beautiful tan face with its fierce, black eyes and perfectly chiseled cheekbones, "you're young, beautiful, intelligent and you're a Christian. Tell me again why you want to marry my brother?" she continued intrepidly, not needing to state the obvious that Bernie was much older than me, had just exited a failed marriage and had a sixteen-year-old son and a twelve-year-old daughter in Dallas waiting for him. When I responded that I was madly in love with her brother, she got even bolder. "I must warn you that Bernie is a very difficult man, and that you're in for a lifetime of serious challenges if you marry him."

"Hedy," I continued very sincerely, "I genuinely believe God has brought me into Bernie's life for the salvation of his soul."

"Okay," she replied, seeing I was unmovable. "I'll be there when you need me, because I can promise you, you're going to need someone to talk to once you're married."

What I failed to mention to her was that I was already three months pregnant with our oldest child and we were in too deep to turn back now. Our daughter Kara was born on Christmas Eve just six months later, and Alexandra, Gabrielle and Christian followed before our fourth anniversary. That was twenty-three years ago now— before life took us to our current home and through an incredible series of trials and tribulations, both marital and familial. And that was when I still believed that life would go according to my hopes, dreams and plans.

Coming Home

Hedy, who turned out to be quite the prophet, ultimately became a dear friend and confidante who led me back home to the Catholic Church four years after I married her brother. Once Bernie and I were married, Hedy started inviting me to her raised, plantation-style house in Pearlington, Mississippi—a little country town that sits on the Pearl River about forty-five minutes east of our home—on a regular basis for her many evangelization outreaches. Though I was still an evangelical Protestant at the time, she never hesitated to include me because she secretly hoped that she could get me, and thus her little nieces, back into the Catholic Church. I, on the other hand, was firmly convinced that Hedy and her Catholic friends were not "saved," and I felt it was my duty to make sure they came to know Jesus Christ. We had several lunch conversations where I took advantage of the opportunity to tell her why the Catholic Church was "wrong" about salvation in teaching that anything besides faith alone is necessary to be saved. "The truth is, all you need to do to be saved is to give your life to Jesus through faith," I told her confidently. "Everything else is a man-made invention."

One day when she'd invited me to her house for a day of prayer, I cornered an elderly priest who had given a talk that day, asking him if he "knew Jesus Christ as his personal Lord and Savior." He just rolled his eyes, and his look told me that an evangelical had hammered him more than once with that question. Though Hedy had to apologize to Father that I had questioned his salvation, she kept inviting me back.

For my part, I kept attending because we had children the same ages and we ended each day by letting all of the children swim in the Pearl River that buttressed their property—rumored to be one of the most alligator-infested rivers in America. On more than one occasion we saw an alligator lurking nearby as the children swam. When I voiced my concern about whether the children were safe, Hedy just responded confidently "The Blessed Mother will keep them safe. No one has ever been hurt on my property because it's consecrated to Mary. And no one is ever going to get hurt here." It turns out she was right about that, too.

The most dramatic evidence of that reality came during Hurricane Katrina, when Hedy's husband Gerry decided not to evacuate for the storm. They, along with their daughter Annie and my mother-in-law Letty, who was eighty-six at the time, wound up on the second floor of the house in life jackets and football helmets as the eye of the hurricane passed directly over their home, bringing a twenty-five-foot storm surge with it. When the hurricane ended, they came downstairs to learn that the tidal wave had completely washed out the first story of their home while they were upstairs, with Hedy praying the Rosary non-stop, all night long. All that was left of the first floor was a mudroom on the back of the house, now occupied by a fifteen-foot alligator that rode the surge into the house. The fact that the structure wasn't completely washed away, like the miles and miles of homes, buildings and casinos along the Mississippi Gulf Coast that simply vanished into Katrina's waters, was nothing short of a miracle. Our Lady did indeed protect the property, just as she protected our home—which is also consecrated to Mary now—from the devastating effects of Katrina.

While I totally embrace devotion to Mary today, I didn't understand it at all in those days. Therefore, whenever we would get in the car to leave, I would inevitably tell my children "We do not worship the Blessed Mother the way Aunt Hedy does, because we are forbidden by the Bible from worshipping anyone but God."

"Yes, Mommy," the children would dutifully reply in unison. "We will never worship the Blessed Mother."

Not surprisingly, it was Hedy and the Blessed Mother who would eventually bring me back into the Catholic Church in 1988, when I was pregnant for our third daughter Gaby. It happened after Hedy invited me to hear a talk given by a member of the Brennan's Restaurant family about a supposed Marian apparition, where the Mother of God was said to be appearing to a group of children with messages for the world.

Though my Protestant pastor had warned me these apparitions were "demonic" and not to touch them with a ten-foot-pole, I heard nothing wrong in the messages, which essentially were an urgent plea to pray, fast and return to God. I bought several books on the topic trying to get a read on the authenticity of the messages, and although I found nothing objectionable in them, I was still genuinely wary about whether Mary could deceive me and lead me away from Jesus. One day in desperation, I prostrated myself on my face on the floor of my bedroom in our home on Kiskatom Lane—only a mile from our current house— begging the Lord to show me if the apparitions were from Him.

"Jesus," I prayed, "if you're sending your mother to this earth with messages for the world, then I want to know. You have GOT to show me if this is from you or if it is from the devil." After getting into bed and falling soundly asleep, I heard what sounded like the door to my bedroom clicking open. I then heard the audible voice of a woman saying clearly: "I will cleanse your family." I sat up immediately in bed, scouring the room to see where the voice had come from, but no one was there. I got out of bed and found Bernie sleeping soundly on the sofa downstairs, where he had fallen asleep watching TV. I didn't sleep another wink that night as I tossed and turned and prayed, not sure what to think about what I'd heard.

In the morning, even more desperate, I prostrated myself on the floor again, begging the Lord to confirm what I took to be the Blessed Mother's voice promising to heal my family, whom I'd been praying for fervently for several years. As I lay on my face on the ground in prayer, the phone rang. It was my brother Kenny calling from Florida, where he had moved several months before. I had not spoken to him since.

"Judy," Kenny began. "I just had to call and tell you that I was walking down the beach and an old, Catholic man came up to me and asked if I knew Jesus Christ as my personal Lord and savior. And I wanted to tell you," he continued "that I knelt down on the beach and prayed to receive Christ as my personal Lord and Savior. I felt the need to call and tell you that." I started crying so hard that I had to hang up the phone, and I fell on the floor again weeping deeply over the incredible and immediate answer to my prayer for confirmation. I returned to the Catholic Church that week, though it would take ten years more years before I really came to understand and embrace what the Catholic Church actually teaches.

One thing that is crystal clear now to me is that the Blessed Mother cannot lead us away from Jesus—she can only point us to Him and tell us "Do whatever He tells you." I love her with all of my heart today and consider myself to be one of her children as I stand with the beloved disciple John at the foot of the Cross heeding Our Lord's words, "Behold, your mother."

Meanwhile, Hedy has been kind enough never to rub it in. She has, however, reminded me many times of Our Lady's prophecy of "cleansing" when I get discouraged about all of the mess in our lives. Though I thought it meant that God would wave a magic wand over my family and me, and with Mary's motherly intercession make everything better instantaneously, I'm beginning to understand that real cleansing is more like a boil erupting than a magic bullet, and that it takes time both to extract the infection from the wound and to repair the damage that's been done. Furthermore, it ain't very pretty when it happens. But neither was the Crucifixion. Salvation has always been a messy business, and the scandal is that God's right there in the midst of all of it.

Hedy's final hurrah in bringing me back to the Catholic faith was to facilitate my study of Catholic theology ten years later in 1998. With her financial help and Bernie's full endorsement, I graduated from the University of Dallas with a Masters Degree in Theological Studies in the Jubilee Year 2000, and have spent every year since then teaching Catholic theology, including serving for the last five years as an Adjunct Professor of Theology at Our Lady of Holy Cross College in New Orleans. My studies have most recently led me to train for a PhD in Bioethics at a pontifical college in Rome, where I am currently enrolled as a student and where I attend classes four weeks per year.

Being a student in Rome for the past two years has afforded me the incredible privilege of spending seventy days of study in the Eternal City—where I've spent much precious time praying, reflecting and weeping. When not in class, I've made use of every available moment to make pilgrimages to holy sites and to the tombs of numerous saints, praying many times for our son Christian at the burial chambers of the indomitable St. Monica, who won her son St. Augustine's hard-fought conversion after her own long years of prayers and tears. I've also ventured repeatedly to the tomb of Pope John Paul II to kneel on the cold marble floor in the crypt beneath St. Peter's Basilica to beg his intercession for our family. I've prayed especially hard there for our daughter Gaby and her unborn son James, whose ultrasound photo a Vatican guard allowed me to place on the great Pope's tomb when he saw me kneeling on the floor in prayer as I held the baby's picture in my hands.

Rome, which is saturated with the blood of Christian saints and martyrs, has been a place of many tears for me since the beautiful fall day of 2006 when I arrived in the city to begin the bioethics program. The first emotional meltdown that I experienced happened on day one of my arrival, when I stepped into St. Peter's Basilica looking for the tomb of Pope John Paul II. Having landed at the airport early on a Sunday morning, I was thrilled to have a day to spend sightseeing before classes began on Monday. I dropped off my things at a friend's apartment where I was staying, then walked to St. Peter's Basilica, which was only blocks away. When I stepped through the church's grand front doors, it literally took my breath away, and a river of tears streamed down my face as I made my way up to the massive front altar while having a vivid flashback of the one and only time I had ever visited the basilica in the past—an event I'd almost completely forgotten.

That earlier visit was during the summer of 1981 when I was living in France on a scholarship that I had won to study at the University of Montpellier, a French-immersion school that sat in a picturesque little beach town on the country's spectacular Mediterranean coast. One weekend, a girlfriend and I decided to take the train to Monaco, where we wound up in a casino at eleven o'clock at night checking out the international high rollers who were gambling there. As we walked out of the casino, we met three super friendly Canadian law students who told us they were getting on the road to Rome and invited us to go with them. Though I would kill my daughters for taking such a foolish risk, we got into their van right then and there and drove all night to Rome, arriving in the city in the wee hours of the morning for a day of sightseeing and Italian food.

The five of us made our way to the Coliseum, and then moved on to St. Peter's Basilica for a dutiful stop in the world's most famous church. It was there that I, an agnostic former Catholic who hadn't set foot in a church in years, unexpectedly stood at the front altar of the awe-inspiring basilica blinking back tears because I could feel the presence of God. I didn't think much of it at the time and tucked it far back into my memory bank, never to ponder it again. At least not until entering the same sacred space some twenty-four years later brought back the same stunning emotion, along with the piercing realization that my adult conversion to Christ had probably begun at that moment years ago when I stood within yards of the bones of the first martyred pope, St. Peter. I was in a crisis of faith then and God somehow brought me to Rome, to the seat of Christianity in the Western world, to beckon me with His powerful presence. And in a new and different crisis of faith a quarter of a century later—one prompted by the mystery of suffering—God has brought me back to Rome once again. At this present time, it feels as though there is a call on my life to mingle my tears with the blood and tears of the martyrs in this holy place.

"The blood of the martyrs is the seedbed of the Church," wrote the Early Church Father and Christian apologist Tertullian in the Third Century. As I walk the streets of Rome today from one holy site to the next, I am constantly reminded that suffering has always been part of the Christian journey, and I pray for a new seeds of faith and hope to spring up within me.

I must confess that the suffering of the past few years— especially the suicides of my two brothers and the death of Bernie's son—has challenged my faith in God at the deepest level that I have experienced

22

since my conversion at age twenty-three. It has, in fact, unearthed a deep dilemma inside of me; namely whether God can really be trusted. I've struggled with trust issues my entire life, spurred on initially by the trauma of childhood sexual abuse at the hands of a distant relative—a wound for which I've sought much therapy and over which I've experienced real healing over the years. But the repeated recent tragedies that have visited our family have torn the scab off the wound of mistrust inside of me, leaving me reeling with hurt and confusion and under heavy assault in my mind that God will not keep me nor my family safe. Although I know in my theologically packed head it's not true and that God is my loving Father, I am wrestling mightily with Him about my life, because it feels like He's out to get me.

"Have I done something to deserve all of this, Lord?" I ask in silent desperation, echoing the accusations of Job's friends, who insisted that he had brought his suffering upon himself through his own wrongdoing. "Though he slay me, yet I will trust in him," I beg God for the grace to pray.

December 22, 2008

I awaken at seven a.m. and remember that Bernie has a stress test planned for tomorrow morning that I must remind him about. Since it's late December and we've met our deductible, his cardiologist suggested that he get the test done before the end of the year. I'm feeling relieved that his elective oral surgery to remove his wisdom teeth, which oddly erupted through his gums at the age of sixty-three, went well last week. And I'll be doubly happy when the stress test is over as well.

To prepare for his dental procedure, the oral surgeon recommended that Bernie stop taking his Plavix, a blood thinner that keeps stents from clotting. Bernie has been taking Plavix for a year, starting when he had four stents inserted in his heart following a minor heart attack last December. Because Plavix can cause bleeding in someone with an open wound, the doctor suggested that Bernie cease using it before the oral surgery. Though Bernie's been off the blood thinner for a week now, I'm not the least bit worried about the possible side effects of stopping the medication. I was more worried about the potential bleeding that could occur when he went under the knife last week to have his teeth removed.

Worrying about Bernie's health has become a regular part of my daily regime during the past year—ever since the 90% blockage in his main artery last December served as a wake-up call that his life could end at any moment. I still remember every detail of that day; starting with the way our then-twenty-two-year-old daughter Kara and I had tried unsuccessfully for two hours to convince him to go to the hospital when he complained of chest pains while watching a Saints game on TV.

Kara, the eldest of our five children together, was home for her birthday and Christmas. We had just returned from the Sunday performance of the Nutcracker Ballet at the St. Joseph Abbey Theater, where we saw Bernie's late son Marshall's thirteen-year-old daughter, Kaylie, dance in the show. Afterward, we went out for a delicious Italian meal at Macaroni Grill, where Bernie had eaten his favorite food of fried calamari. Not long after, we were enjoying a relaxing evening in the den watching a Saints game when Bernie started complaining that his chest was hurting. Insistent that it was only indigestion from the fried calamari he'd eaten, my stubborn husband finally agreed to seek medical assistance when he broke out in a cold, clammy sweat and Kara issued him an ultimatum: "Get in the car or I'm calling 9-1-1!" He reluctantly agreed to come with us, but not without watching "one more play." When we arrived

24

at the Emergency Room, he had normal blood pressure, normal cholesterol and a normal EKG in spite of the fact that he was having a heart attack. Typical Bernie!

After the on-call cardiologist's assessment, we were offered two options: a quadruple heart bypass or stents. As the recovery from the quadruple bypass would cause a cancellation of our planned family Christmas trip to New York City two weeks later—where Kara was scheduled to sing at Carnegie Hall!—we both agreed that stents were the best option. Besides, we agreed, it was a no-brainer that the least invasive surgery made the most sense.

Kara, who is a gifted singer, songwriter, and chastity speaker, lives in L.A. and travels around the country giving concerts and "chastity talks" to teens. A deeply sensitive and spiritual person from the time she was a little girl, Kara is passionate about sharing her love of God with others, and especially about empowering young women to remain sexually pure before marriage. Two weeks after she left for college in 2004 at The Catholic University of America in Washington, D.C., her half-brother Marshall—Bernie's eldest of the two children from his first marriage—died. The anxiety and stress took such a toll on her that she decided to take a leave of absence from school, and she's been traveling around the country singing and ministering to the youth since then, while finishing her B.A. in Education online.

Sadly, every time she comes home, we seem to be in a new crisis. I know full well that all of the family chaos produces intense anxiety in Kara, which is evident by her chewed-bare fingernails. Being that she's the oldest of our five children, she feels a particular responsibility for the wellbeing of our family, and she carries our difficulties on her back like a heavy leaden cross. That has been especially true concerning her little brother Christian, who has had a rather rough go of it in life thus far.

Christian Bernard, while being one of the sweetest, most talented and most beautiful human beings that I have ever known, has been in and out of trouble since he was barely a teen. The first intervention we ever did on him was at the tender age of thirteen—just two weeks after Marshall died—when we sent him to live on a youth ranch in Wyoming for a year after learning that he'd been sneaking out of the house at night for several months wreaking havoc in our neighborhood with several other boys. At the time, we figured that relocating him to the wilderness of Wyoming would spare him from going down a dangerous, destructive path. But I second-guess that decision constantly now, especially as our youngest son

Benjamin approaches the pre-teens and I realize that a boy that age is practically a baby.

Christian has been the apple of Bernie's eye since the day he was born in September 1990—the day Bernie appointed the newborn as "prince" of our family. "You see this boy," he said to me and our four, three and one-year-old little daughters as he held the baby high in the air mimicking a scene from one of his all-time favorite movies. "He's in charge! That's the way it's done in Latin families!" Bernie continued with a huge grin on his face, thoroughly amused with himself. Though I thought he was joking at the time, I would come to learn that IS the way it's done in Latin families, and that a totally different standard exists for the boys and girls in a family.

Bernie's putting Christian "in charge" meant that Christian was allowed to do whatever he wanted, with Bernie's favorite mantra for him becoming "give him whatever he wants!" But when Bernie had enough of Christian's antics, he would rage out on the child with fury, causing me to come to Christian's defense and, as Bernie saw it, undermine his authority. Needless to say, Christian's being put "in charge" would lead to World War III between Bernie and me, as I strove unsuccessfully to discipline and then defend the child while Bernie reprimanded me constantly for both correcting Christian and protecting him. Tragically, the poor kid became the battleground on which a seemingly endless power struggle in our marriage played out, and I can't help but wonder if that's driven the boy to the brink.

"No wonder the kid's in a rehab facility," I think, blaming both Bernie and myself for this fiasco. But no amount of regret can change things now.

Unfortunately, there's no changing or hiding the fact that our family is a complete mess, or that Bernie and I are at our wits end from all of the problems in our lives. It's also plain as day that Bernie has visibly declined since four years ago when Marshall died and we sent Christian to live in Wyoming within a two-week time span. The poor man cried so much that year I feared his heart would break. I wasn't terribly surprised when he finally had a heart attack a year ago, as it seemed to me at the time to be a tangible sign of his suffering.

Though Bernie had been healthy as a horse and driven as the wind his whole life, he's clearly not the same man these days. Instead of enthusiastically sharing with me the details of every new deal he's concocting, he prefers to spend his time quietly picking the heads off the roses in our garden or playing Sudoku in the courtyard when he's not at work. Many a night he sits until the wee hours of the morning playing endless rounds of Solitaire on the computer, attempting to beat back the stress of life through mindless game playing.

Though Bernie survived his heart attack with no residual heart damage, between his health issues, the kids' problems and my brothers' and Marshall's deaths, I've become increasingly aware of how tenuous life can be. I find myself struggling with feeling unsafe and uncertain about the future more and more lately as I live on high alert, waiting for the hammer to fall. The days of taking life for granted are gone and I worry daily about Bernie having another episode with his heart, or about getting a phone call that someone we love has died. I live with the sinking feeling that something terrible is getting ready to happen, and I practice surrendering Bernie, the kids and our lives to God over and over again. I assure myself there's nothing to worry about tomorrow. It's just a simple stress test—right? I get out of bed and make a mental note to remind Bernie about his appointment.

The Perfect Storm

December 23, 2008

8:00 a.m.

It's eight o'clock the next morning when our daughter Gaby enters the kitchen where I'm finishing a double cappuccino. "Mom, I've been having contractions every five minutes for the past two hours," she announces. "One woke me up from a dead sleep it was so strong," she continues with tears in her eyes. "I think we'd better go to the hospital."

Gabrielle, our third daughter and "baby girl," is nineteen and expecting her first child. I affectionately nicknamed Gaby our "Latin child" when she was just a baby because people kept asking me what country I'd adopted her from. Apparently, she looked like a foreigner in my arms with her big black eyes and dark skin, which were quite the contrast to my blonde, Germanic looks. Now people tell me that she looks like the movie star Eva Mendes, and I have to agree, she does. Because of her exotic beauty and fiery Latin personality, which reminds Bernie of himself, she has always held a special place in her daddy's heart. Bernie has made no secret of that fact since the day she was born and my sister Joanne announced after her delivery: "Wow! She's darker than the other two girls and she looks more like Bernie than both of them!"

"Okay, baby, let me get my suitcase packed," I quickly respond to the tearful mama-to-be. "Dad left to have his stress test done, so he and the rest of the family can meet us in New Orleans after the midwife confirms you're in active labor."

I throw a couple of things into an overnight bag and hurriedly get dressed. As we live in a suburb forty-five minutes from the hospital, I don't want to take any chances that my daughter will have the baby on the twenty-four-mile-long Causeway Bridge, known as "the longest bridge in the world"—that is, until recently when the Chinese beat us out for the record.

We pile into the car, where I double-check to make sure we have all the supplies Gaby prepared for her planned natural birth. "Have you got the pillow for the tub, the Gatorade, the yoga ball and the music you want to listen to?" I ask Gaby, making sure we have gathered all of the things that the midwife suggested to help her get through the labor. "Got it," she says. "Have you got the baby's coming home outfit?" I query. "Got it," she answers again. "What about the hose for the tub?" I ask. Gaby plans to have a bathtub in her labor and delivery room, and we were instructed to bring a hose to fill it up. "Grayson's picking that up on the way to the hospital," she responds.

Grayson, our soon-to-be-born-grandson's father, is a twenty-year-old college student who has moved into our house during Christmas break to assist with the birth of his first son. I pray that Grayson will take good care of James and thus far, I have no reason to believe otherwise. Grayson and his family have proven themselves to be wonderful people and his parents, Bunny and Jay, are clearly invested in being involved in their grandchild's life. They have rallied with us to give James Gabriel a heartfelt welcome when he arrives into the world, and are even driving from South Carolina to be present at the hospital when he is born.

Gaby and I get on the Causeway, and as I time her contractions and try to keep her calm and soothed, she asks very seriously, "Why didn't you tell me this hurts so much!?" I answer without hesitation, working to keep a straight face. "Why do you think I had five epidurals?" I instruct her to practice her "most relaxing breath" just the way we rehearsed it in birthing class. I'm her labor coach and I fret about whether I will remember all of the techniques we learned in class to distract her from the pain, such as holding ice on your skin until it hurts or staring at an object on the ceiling until the rest of the world disappears.

Though I'm a little nervous about losing my composure when things get intense, I take comfort in the fact that both of the midwives are trained "doulas" or birthing coaches that lots of women hire to assist them through labor and delivery. They're experts at this business. I take less comfort in the fact that I was the type of mother who couldn't insert a suppository into my children's behinds when they were sick without giggling hysterically. Somehow the sight of a rear end propped in the air for the delivery of a suppository seemed absurdly funny to me in the middle of a sleepless night. I'm actually worried that I may start giggling uncontrollably at the most inappropriate time, but thankfully, if I do, the doulas will be there to take over.

We arrive in the city finally and pull up in front of the midwives' office, which is directly across the street from Touro hospital—the same hospital where Bernie's eldest daughter Kerry, who was twelve when we married, was rehabilitated for six months (another trauma!) after suffering a serious head injury during a car accident on New Year's Eve a dozen years ago. Though Kerry miraculously recuperated fully, I will never forget coming into our bedroom closet to tell Bernie the corned beef, cabbage, and black-eyed peas were ready to find him doubled over on the floor crying hysterically after receiving "the phone call" no parent ever wants to get.

"Your daughter has had an accident," the state trooper said. "You need to get to the hospital immediately because they don't know if she'll survive."

Though we had been married over ten years at the time, I had never seen Bernie cry. I had seen him get angry and throw lots of other intense emotions around, but I had never once seen him cry. It was heart wrenching to watch his floodgate of tears burst open, and to witness him crying like a baby for months after Kerry's accident almost every place he went, including business meetings. He simply could not get a hold of himself. The cure for his crying finally came nearly a year later when he broke down during a meeting in front of his brother, Henry, and some clients. Henry, who is an attorney and was representing Bernie in a business deal, pulled him aside and scolded him sternly saying, "What the hell is wrong with you? Get a grip on yourself and never cry at a meeting again!"

That brotherly admonition jolted the floodgates closed and they stayed closed until we received "the other phone call" from Marshall's wife, Lisa, ten years later, on Labor Day of 2004. The thirty-year-old couple and their two little girls had moved near us to a home in Beau Chene five years earlier, when Marshall left his job at a sales rep for a heavy equipment company in Michigan to start a Louisiana-based internet business and locate his young family closer to relatives.

"You need to come to the hospital immediately because Marshall is very sick," Lisa told us with a shaky voice. "The doctor said his liver is failing and he's in critical condition," she continued.

Marshall was in a coma by the time we arrived at the hospital, and the doctors declared him brain dead five days later. I have never witnessed anything so devastatingly painful as watching Bernie and his ex-wife Marsha say goodbye to their son before his life support was disconnected. How much heartache can two people possibly handle? I wondered as I stood watching these two parents stand together over a child's hospital bed once again, traumatically reconnected a second time by a tragic turn of events. Bernie never stopped crying after that.

Many nights since then I've awaked to the shaking of the mattress to find my broken husband crying quietly but convulsively in the darkness. All I can do is put my arms around him and cry with him, and I can feel his broken heart. Bernie can't forgive himself for Marshall's death, for which he blames himself. Due to some dreadful financial decisions Bernie made when he and Marshall were starting a company together five years before in 1999, their relationship had become severely strained. But the straw that broke the camel's back had been the day Marshall found out that Bernie had filed for a decree of nullity for his first marriage. I'll never forget that day, either.

Bernie and I were walking into the our parish church for our son Christian's First Holy Communion when we spotted Marshall talking to the deacon and approached the two of them to say hello. Deacon Rudy, who assumed Marshall knew, announced loudly to all of us: "When your father gets his annulment, the two of you can get married in the Church at the same time!" Marshall and Lisa had been meeting with the same deacon to discuss the possibility of having their marriage blessed in the Church, as Lisa was in the process of converting to Catholicism at the time. But Bernie had been waiting for the right time to inform his two older children about the annulment, because he was convinced they weren't going to take it well. When the deacon dropped that bomb, Marshall looked like he had seen a ghost. He then proceeded to run like hell out of the church, jump into his car and speed off out of the church parking lot.

When the First Communion service concluded, we returned to our home with my parents, who were crushed and fragile after having buried my thirty-five-year-old brother Scott to suicide a mere week earlier. As Bernie sat on the back deck comforting my poor weeping father, Marshall ran through the house demanding to speak to him. Though Bernie tried to calm him down as they walked to the front of the house, Marshall was devastated and inconsolable at what he perceived as the final and ultimate betrayal—his father's petition for a decree of nullity for his marriage to his mother. We watched Marshall ran like fire out of the house and burn rubber in the street as he departed, driving away with all of the passion and fury of a tender-hearted son whose lifetime of hurts had been pushed over the edge by this latest round of news.

Marshall didn't see or speak to his father for the next five years, and it was only a miracle of grace that reconciled them just two weeks before Marshall's death. That reconciliation came about as a result of our eldest daughter Kara, who was eighteen at the time and releasing her first CD. When Marshall heard about the CD, he called Kara and offered to design a website for her, as he had started an incredibly successful Internet company and knew he could help her out. In her young wisdom, Kara said, "Marshall, you have to talk to Dad about this. He is my manager and you really need to arrange this through him."

"Fine," said Marshall "you two come to my office next week and we'll have a meeting about it."

Though Bernie was elated by this opportunity to see his son again, the disappointment set in when Marshall sent in his web design team to conduct the meeting instead of coming in personally. When the meeting ended, Bernie found Marshall in the hall and asked "Can I please speak to you alone?" Marshall agreed and in they went into his private office, where his shattered son cried bitterly as Bernie begged forgiveness for the many hurts he had inflicted during Marshall's life. Bernie came home glowing and humbled as he recounted their conversation, but he was very concerned about his son's health.

"Judy," he told me, "I've always known when something's wrong with Marshall since the time he was a little boy, and I'm telling you that boy is sick."

They would have one more meeting before we got "the call" telling us that Marshall was comatose due to sudden liver failure. Bernie has never been the same, and I have a whole new appreciation of what people mean when they say that you never recover from the death of a child.

December 23, 2008

11:00 a.m.

Gaby and I park in front of Touro Hospital, and I remind myself that this time we're arriving here for a happy event. I'm all too aware that the sights and smells of particular places have a way of bringing back intense memories, and Bernie is liable to break down crying when he gets here. We've never driven past this place since Kerry's accident without at least a mention of her stay here, along with a wave of anxiety over the memory of her accident and head injury.

Entering the midwife's office, Gaby is greeted happily in the lobby by the nurse midwife named Kathy, who's on call today and hopes to deliver James. Nurse Kathy has flattered and blessed Gaby throughout the pregnancy by making much over how beautiful and special she is. "I think I'm her favorite patient," Gaby beams proudly every time she returns home from an appointment. My mother's heart appreciates her kindness more than words can say, and I'm grateful that my young daughter feels confident about herself and her baby every time she returns from seeing the midwife.

Sadly, I have been unable to offer much emotional support to Gaby at this moment in her life, due to my own preoccupation with the sorrow and suffering in our lives. When she came into the house last May to tell us she was expecting, I told her she'd have to break the news to her dad herself. Though I wasn't quite sure what to expect from Bernie, he reacted beautifully to Gaby's announcement. "Baby, it's okay. You're not going to do this alone. I am going to support you every step of the way." After we exchanged a few more sentences, he stood up, gave our daughter a big bear hug and walked out.

As Bernie went back outside to finish constructing a gate for our garbage yard, it hit me like a ton of bricks that, in one instant, our lives had just dramatically changed again. And with that, Bernie seemed to pass the "crying bug" to me, and MY floodgate of tears erupted. I have cried what seems like buckets of tears over the past few months—worrying incessantly about my daughter and her baby and whether they will be all right. My tears for Gaby piggyback on my tears for Christian, whose escalating addiction has made his life, and ours, completely unmanageable. "This is SOOOO not what I had planned for my life," becomes my mantra.

33

"Why is everything always about you?" Gaby asks angrily as the months pass and my crying continues. "You are acting like a total victim, as usual!" she says. And she's right. I feel totally victimized by my life at this point. It feels like a battering ram to me.

Though I'm trying to learn that there is a God and it's not me, the repeated lesson of surrendering my expectations about life has been a hard one, and I've cried bitter tears as the realization has sunk in that not only am I not in control of anything, I'm completely out of control most of the time. "When and how did I buy into the lie that if I did "X" and "Y" I was going to get "Z" result?" I ask myself constantly. I have believed that if I try hard enough, love hard enough, pray hard enough and, of course, get enough therapy, I will produce a different result in my children than my parents produced in my own "dysfunctional" family of origin—and that my children will therefore not become drug addicts like my brothers or get pregnant out of wedlock like me. It's been humbling to learn the hard way that life is just plain old messy and painful. And there ain't no guarantees.

"I'm a victim," I often mumble to myself in private. "Maybe I should do what Job's wife suggested and just curse God and die." With drama and trauma all around me, all year I'd been thinking about throwing in the towel on this whole Christianity thing, because I certainly hadn't signed up for this much suffering. Luckily, before I had the chance to abandon my faith completely, my sister-in-law Hedy had invited me to attend a healing retreat a month ago in November. I figured that Gaby could use the retreat as much as I, so I'd signed us both up.

A seasoned exorcist named Fr. Jerry Drinkwater had led the three-day retreat, held at the beautiful St. Augustine Seminary retreat center a block from Gulf of Mexico in Bay St. Louis Mississippi. As the retreat began, Fr. Jerry asked for a volunteer and my hand shot up. Father asked me to sit in the center of the circle where all seventy-five attendees had gathered.

"What mask have you been wearing your whole life that you would like to take off this weekend?" he asked me.

Though I was thinking of saying something else completely, the words that came out of my mouth were "I'm a victim. I've been a victim my whole life and I'm tired of it!" The next thing I knew, all seventy-five people were praying over me while I cried feverishly in the center of the circle. Gaby had stepped out of the room for five minutes to go to the bathroom, only to return to her "victim" mother weeping uncontrollably in

34

the middle of the room. As she rolled her eyes and sat down, I shared the details of the tragedies in our lives with the entire group.

"My brothers both committed suicide due to drug addiction, and my last brother who died killed his wife too," I lamented. "My stepson died suddenly at thirty-six and I'm afraid my son will be next," I continued. "There's a spirit of death coming after the men in this family and I want it stopped!" I cried with righteous anger.

After praying over me for a while, Fr. Jerry announced his plans to change the retreat program so that the weekend could focus completely on healing prayer for my family and me. "Girl, you've got problems," the old exorcist said without saying it. "You need a miraculous intervention!"

I can only say that by the grace of God, I was delivered that weekend from believing the lie that I was a victim—a deeply held conviction that had gained a stronghold in my soul early on in life through the trauma of sexual abuse. That belief, which had driven many of the decisions I had made in life and determined to a great extent how I viewed God and reality, was miraculously healed as Fr. Jerry and the retreat participants prayed for me.

As the weekend concluded, a woman praying over me had a most beautiful vision for my future. "I see you dressed as a warrior, like Joan of Arc," she prophesied. "You will no longer be a victim but a VICTOR and you will know the victory of Jesus Christ in your life!" Those glorious words were music to my ears, and I received them happily and headed for home renewed, refreshed and encouraged. Little did I know that God was equipping me to fight the toughest battle of my life—the battle for Bernie's life and his soul.

December 23, 2008

11:30 a.m.

As Nurse Kathy escorts Gaby to the back examination room, I park myself on a lounger in the waiting room wondering if she's dilated the six centimeters we'd hoped for in the car. A few minutes later, she returns to the front room with a long face, quite obviously disappointed with the news. "One centimeter, that's it. Kathy said to go find somewhere comfortable to rest for a while before checking into the hospital, because we're in for a long haul."

We decide on my mother's home, as it's just a few blocks away. "We'll go rest at Maw Maw's and come back in a couple of hours to see if you've progressed," I say in my most reassuring voice. Minutes later, we arrive at my mother's house, a one story brick ranch-style home that sits among the mansions on St. Charles Avenue, one of the most well-known streets in New Orleans. Though we were raised in a large, stucco home in a newer area of the city known as Gentilly, which is about fifteen minutes away, my mother's dream to live on St. Charles Avenue—smack dab on the parade route for the Mardi Gras parades which she loves—was realized when all ten children had finally left the nest.

We take a long walk around her Garden District neighborhood, passing the home of vampire author Anne Rice and the family home of football superstars Peyton and Eli Manning as we attempt to hasten the arrival of the baby. Around noon, we settle into the back bedroom of the house nervously to hunker down and wait for active labor.

As we time another contraction and fill up another cup of Gatorade, my cell phone rings identifying the caller as "Hubby." I answer the phone to give Bernie an update on Gaby's labor, only to hear a distressed voice on the other line with news of, almost unbelievably, yet another trauma.

"Judy, I'm having a heart attack! I just called 9-1-1!" It's now 12:30 and Bernie, who is home, just finished his stress test thirty minutes ago.

"Jesus, Mary and Joseph!" I exclaim as I look blankly at Gaby. Though I'm a devout Catholic, I've inherited my mother's favorite exclamatory phrase for every crisis, and I assure myself that it counts as a prayer because I love the three of them so much. "I'm going to call Jill to come from next door right away. She's a nurse and I'll ask her to sit with you until the ambulance arrives."

"Okay," Bernie says panting for breath. "Hurry! This is bad! I'm in terrible pain."

"Just hang on," I tell him anxiously, "I'm calling Jill right now." I quickly call and arrange for my neighbor to go to our house then I look up at my mother momentarily, feeling nothing but total panic and confusion.

"Bernie's having a heart attack and Gaby's in labor...I don't know what to do!" I say worriedly, feeling pulled between my commitment to serve as my daughter's labor coach and the pressing need to be with my husband. "Judy, go with your husband! Gaby will be okay," Mama commands with the firm confidence of a woman who delivered ten kids in eleven years. Suddenly, it is obvious to me that, of course, that's what I should do. I kiss my daughter goodbye and tell her I'll try to be back in time for the delivery, thinking this will be like last time and all Bernie will need is a couple of new stents. But knowing that the hospital is near our home forty-five minutes away, I silently realize it's quite possible that I'll miss the delivery of the baby completely.

As I cross the Causeway in the opposite direction trying to pray and stay calm, Jill assures me by phone that they made it to the hospital and everything is okay. "Drive carefully," she tells me, "and don't speed. I'll wait here until you get here."

I park the car near the Emergency Room and run into my second hospital today as fast as I can. I find Jill in the hall, who points me toward the doctors running Bernie's stretcher down the hallway toward the Operating Room.

"They need you to sign consent forms for surgery," she says. "They're going to do a by-pass right away."

Having reviewed the options carefully last December after Bernie's first heart attack, I know that by-pass surgery is far more invasive than the stent procedure we opted for. Bernie was hesitant at the time to have his "virgin" chest cracked open, but now he would have no choice. I say goodbye to Jill and run down the corridor toward the stretcher, where I find the cardiologist who has treated Bernie since last December.

"Dr. Madden, what the hell happened?" I ask frankly, surprised at the aggression in my voice. "Bernie just finished his stress test at noon!" The words sound like an accusation, but I can't help myself.

"Was he taking his Plavix?" Dr. Madden asks immediately trying to assess the situation.

"No, he stopped taking it a week ago to have his oral surgery done."

"Oh my God," he responds nervously as his face turns ashen. "I would have never let him set foot on that treadmill if I'd known he was off his Plavix!"

"Dr. Madden, you signed off on it," I respond in complete disbelief, wondering how that critical information could have fallen through the cracks.

"I need you to sign the consent forms for open heart surgery," Madden says quickly. "You can sit in the waiting room and I'll come get you as soon as possible to tell you what we've found."

I wander aimlessly down the hallway toward the Surgery Waiting Room, but when I see the large crowd inside I decide to pull a chair out into the hall to sit alone. I am far too nervous to share a space with others, and somehow, the open corridor connecting the thoroughfares of the hospital seems more private than the Waiting Room. I'm relieved when I see my old friend Cecil and her husband Johnny, who's a doctor here, walking toward me, obviously aware of what has happened. They came immediately when they heard the news that an ambulance had been at our house.

Cecil and I have been friends for twenty-five years, ever since the day we met at that little evangelical Christian church on Tulane University's campus in New Orleans where I gave my life to Christ. We had four babies together, and though she went on to have her fifth child without me, I would eventually catch up when I had our fifth nine years later at the age of thirty-nine. I'll always remember her screaming at the top of her lungs in jubilation when I called to tell her I was pregnant. That unbridled display of fervor over the news, along with her conversion to Catholicism, earned her the right to become Benjamin Joseph's godmother.

I had returned to the Catholic Church in 1988 when I was pregnant with Gaby, and truly caught the fervor of what Pope John Paul II called the "New Evangelization" nine years later when I began studying Catholic theology. Though Cecil and I had several tense conversations about the Catholic faith as my studies intensified, she showed up at my house one day with hat in hand asking for me to give her "all of the arguments in favor of the Catholic Church." We met in my home for weeks thereafter while I shared with her much of the information I had gathered supporting the biblical foundation of Catholicism. As I had read every apologetics book I could get my hands on, I knew she didn't have a prayer.

"Apologetics does not mean apologizing to people that we are Catholic," I explained during our first meeting. "It means being able to give a reasonable and biblically-based defense for our faith, especially when we are challenged about Catholic beliefs and practices." I then covered a series of topics with her including "Scripture Alone," "Faith Alone," "Purgatory," and "Papal Infallibility," along with other subjects that have been hotly contested by Protestants and grossly misunderstood by Catholics, including me.

"There are not more than one hundred people in the world who truly hate the Catholic Church, but there are millions who hate what they perceive to be the Catholic Church," Bishop Fulton Sheen once famously said. Though Cecil never hated the Church, I jumped at the chance to clear up a lot of misunderstandings.

Cecil entered the Catholic Church with all five of her children at the Easter Vigil in the Jubilee Year 2000. It was probably the most beautiful liturgy I have ever attended and I'm still in awe over the miracle.

December 23, 2008

1:30 p.m.

As Cecil and Johnny approach me in the hall outside the surgery waiting room, I am agitated and angry at what appears to me to be a comedy of errors.

"Who has their flippin' wisdom teeth removed at age sixty-three? And how did Bernie wind up with a stress test ordered just because we'd met our deductible? And while he was off his Plavix, nonetheless! How ridiculous can this be?" I ask Cecil furiously. "And why didn't he take better care of himself after his heart attack?"

My head whirls with questions and accusations while Johnny assures me he will go into the surgical area to see what he can find out. Cecil agrees to sit with me and wait, so we pull another chair out into the hall and promptly join hands and begin to pray. "Lord Jesus," Cecil prays out loud "we ask you to heal Bernie's heart and give the doctors the wisdom to know exactly how to treat him. And we ask that you send your angels into that operating room right now to surround Bernie and protect him." While we are still praying, Johnny returns to report that he has spoken to Bernie, who was awake and alert, and that the doctor has everything under control. He and Cecil have to leave and I hug them goodbye, thanking them for coming.

Minutes later, I spot Dr. Madden coming through the double doors that lead to the surgery area. As our eyes make contact, I brace myself for the news.

"Bernie's okay," he reports. "We didn't need to do a bypass because I was able to reopen the stent that we put in last year in the main artery of his heart. It was completely closed." Shaking his head, he continues, "Judy, I have absolutely no explanation for why Bernie is alive. The stent in Bernie's main artery was 100% occluded and he had no blood flow to 75% of his heart. He had a massive heart attack called 'the widow maker' that usually kills people within three minutes. He's very lucky that he survived such an enormous insult to his heart. I've got the blood flowing through his arteries, but he's still in very critical condition. I've sent him to the ICU and it will take several days for us to determine how much permanent heart damage he has. You can come in and see him as soon as we get him settled."

The words "permanent heart damage" bang like loud drums in my ears. This is the first time it has even occurred to me that Bernie's heart might be damaged, or that there could be serious repercussions to this day's events. Though I feel myself getting panicky at what permanent heart damage might mean, I push that thought away, as it's too much for me to assimilate right now. I'll cross that bridge when I get to it, I think. I just need to get to the ICU to see Bernie right now. As I walk down the hall toward intensive care, my cell phone begins to ring.

"Mom, how's Dad? Did he have open heart surgery?" Gaby asks, responding to the news she heard via my brief phone call to my mother when I first arrived at the hospital.

"No, thank God," I try to assure her. "The doctor was able to open the stent in the main artery of Dad's heart and avoid doing open heart surgery. It was 100% closed. The bad news is that he may have some damage to his heart. They need to run some tests over the next few days to see how his heart looks. He's in critical condition and I'm just going in to see him. How are you, baby?" I ask, worried about her and the baby, feeling awful that she's trying to deliver her first child with her father in critical condition and her mother missing in action.

"I'm still having contractions every five minutes, and I'm getting exhausted," she says in a weepy voice. "I'm at Maw Maw's with Grayson, Jo Jo, Kara and Alex. Jo Jo thinks I need to come back across the lake to deliver the baby. Are you coming back here? Do you think I should switch hospitals?" she asks.

My sister Joanne, affectionately known as "Jo Jo," has arrived at my mother's house and taken charge of the situation there, and I'm greatly relieved to know she's on hand to help Gaby. Being eighteen months older than I in a lineup of ten kids, Jo Jo has always been a second mother to my five children and me. As our own mother had ten children under eleven— we were numbers five and six respectively—the older siblings had to watch out for the younger ones. I was the baby girl, and somehow Jo Jo assumed the role of being responsible for me.

We still laugh until our sides split when I tell the story of how Jo Jo pulled out her Girl Scout knife to protect me from some hoodlums who chased us for several blocks through our Gentilly neighborhood on the way home from St. James Major Church one night. Because I couldn't run fast enough to keep up with her athletic stride, she was forced to stop fleeing and confront the aggressors, threatening them at knifepoint and

41

swearing to God that she'd "kill them if they took one step closer." That was classic Jo Jo. I have always envied her grit. She has never been afraid to step up to the front lines to protect her loved ones with the fearlessness of a mother lion, and she is equally prone to spoil her cubs with reckless abandon whenever the opportunity presents itself. My children and I have often been the lucky recipients of both her protection and her generosity, and we've long accepted the fact that she's going to get involved in all of our affairs.

At this moment, Jo Jo is apparently lobbying to have Gaby abandon her birth plan at Touro and come to Northlake Hospital where Bernie and I are. I'm secretly grateful for her interference, as I would never have had the nerve to suggest such a thing myself. So when my daughter asks, "What do you think, Mom? Should I come to Northlake to deliver the baby there with you?" all I can say is "Oh my gosh, sweetie, I couldn't begin to ask you to do that," knowing that whomever is on call will deliver the baby, and that "whomever" might implement all sorts of interventions Gaby didn't plan for and worse, was adamantly opposed to.

Jo Jo has always been the strong one, the decisive one. I, on the other hand, am "the most indecisive person the world has ever seen," according to my husband, who has told me that at least a thousand times.

"You survey people before you make a decision," Bernie frequently tells me, frustrated by my indecision and by the way other people's opinions can sway me from one position to the other. Right now, I'm incapable of deciding anything, especially something as important as who's going to deliver my daughter's baby.

"No," I tell Gaby. "You and Jo Jo decide what to do. I cannot make that decision for you." I am completely inundated with Bernie's health crisis at the moment, and if I have to make an important decision like that right now, I might implode.

I hang up the phone and head toward the ICU, where the nurses greet me and tell me Bernie is alert and waiting to see me. As I enter his room, I see my husband lying there looking overwhelmed and out of control—totally out of character for his Type A, high control personality. I put on my most chipper voice and try to look calm.

"Hi, honey," I manage to say, "How are you?"

42

He rolls his eyes, shakes his head and sighs deeply, making a typical Bernie face. "The doctor said I had a massive heart attack. Crap! I can't even believe this." Looking up at me he continues, "You don't look too upset." At the mention of those words, I lose my composure and begin to cry.

"I'm trying not to cry so you won't be scared," I say blinking back tears. As I hold his hand and sit next to the bed, I feel a seismic shift in reality. It is beginning to sink in that my husband may be very sick, and I suddenly have the sensation that I'm teetering on the edge of Mt. Everest trying not to fall off. I try to reassure Bernie that everything is going to be okay, but I'm not sure I believe it. Moments later, Dr. Madden enters the room.

"Okay, Bernie, tell me what happened. You came to see me two weeks ago and you were feeling fine. Did you start having symptoms after that?" Dr. Madden asks.

"Feeling fine?!!!" I interrupt incredulously. "Honey, I made the appointment with Dr. Madden because you were having chest pains! Didn't you tell the doctor you were having chest pains?" I demand in a voice that betrays my frustration.

"I wasn't having any chest pains that day," Bernie offers with his usual boyish grin. "So no, I didn't tell him."

"Holy crap, Bernie," I reply tersely, feeling the anger rising within me at his insanity-producing habit of refusing to address anything until it becomes a full-blown crisis. "How could you not have told the doctor you were having chest pains? What could you have been thinking? You told me Dr. Madden said you were fine and that you were probably ready to get off your medication completely," I continue.

"Are you going to bust my behind?!" Bernie retorts, moving into the defensive mode. "What do you want me to do about it now?!" Bernie and I have never minced words when speaking to each other, and today is no exception.

"Okay, okay, you guys," interrupts Dr. Madden, entering the dialogue like a trained referee. "Bernie, you are going to need a chaperone from now on when you come to my office so we can make sure the communication is clear between us. But for now, we're going to get an ultrasound of your heart to see how much damage it has sustained.

Generally, after a massive heart attack, one of two things will happen. Either the damaged area of the heart will begin to start pumping again or the heart will go into cardiogenic shock and the patient will go into congestive heart failure. Let's hope and pray that the second scenario doesn't happen. We'll see how things look on the ultrasound."

As Madden moves to the side to let the ultrasound technician in, I have the sinking feeling that we are not only in a serious crisis, but very probably a life-threatening one. The words "congestive heart failure" have brought a new dimension of gravity to this situation, and I anxiously watch the technician wheel in the big machine with its dark screen, pull up Bernie's gown, and squirt gooey jelly all over his chest. He places the prod on Bernie's chest and slides it up, down and sideways over his heart. It is plain as day to me and to the medical personnel that most of Bernie's heart is not moving, while a small section of the heart is still pumping steadily. After what seems like an eternity of watching the monitor, Dr. Madden finally speaks.

"Yeah," the young cardiologist observes while nodding his head, "that's exactly what I saw in surgery. About 75% of his heart is not pumping. Let's hope that improves overnight. We'll do another ultrasound tomorrow morning and hopefully his heart will have started to rebound."

I'm always amazed at the different ways people digest bad news. For some of us, it's sort of like swallowing a tough, half-chewed piece of meat, which we quadrant off in small sections that we think we're capable of ingesting. This morning I was excitedly taking my daughter across the lake to welcome a precious new member of our family into the world, eagerly awaiting holding a perfect newborn infant in my arms. Now I'm standing next to my critically ill husband's hospital bed feeling like I'm chewing on dry sand that won't go down my throat.

I'm trying to process what has happened today, but I can't take it in. All I can feel is that gnawing sensation that things in our life continually go from bad to worse, and that thought sends me into a state of panic that makes me want to throw up my white flag at God screaming "Uncle, already! I give!!!! Call off the dogs!" Truth be told, that desperate prayer is the one I've prayed the most over the last several years.

I sit with Bernie for the rest of the evening in his ICU cell, intermittently fielding phone calls from our children and various other family members. My sister Renee, who was a nurse for many years in New Orleans, has come and gone in an attempt to get a read on Bernie's medical condition and bring a report back to the rest of the family. Jo Jo has moved with the entire birthing party, which consists of herself, Grayson, Kara, and Alexandra, to her house in Old Metairie, a suburb on the Southshore about fifteen minutes outside of New Orleans. She has assigned Kara and Alex as surrogate birthing coaches, and they're sitting with their little sister as she takes a warm bath, trying to soothe her never-ending contractions.

While Kara nervously chews her nails, Alex looks pale and worried, just as she's been throughout most of the family crises we have endured. She often "takes on" our family drama, and this moment in life is no exception. Alex, who has a sensitive and compassionate heart, has been personally invested in everyone's pain since she was a little girl—so much so that we began to call her "the public defender" when she was very young. If someone else got in trouble, she cried. If someone got a spanking, she cried even harder. I was amazed to learn as I stood in the Christian bookstore one day perusing a book on the meaning of names that "Alexandra" means "defender of mankind." I became convinced that day that God chooses our names for us and that they are very specific to our calling in life.

At nine p.m., Jo Jo makes the executive decision that Gaby will, in fact, come to Northlake for the delivery, as Bernie's condition is very critical, and it has become increasingly obvious that neither he nor I are leaving the hospital any time soon. The whole exhausted clan begins making their way back across the Causeway, while Gaby's contractions continue to present themselves every five minutes. At last check, she is not even in active labor yet. The poor child is dog-tired and all she wants to do is get in her bed and get some sleep. The midwife has given her some medicine that will either "help her sleep or bring on active labor." I assure her by phone that I'll meet her at home as soon as visiting hours are over, and at ten p.m., I kiss my husband's face, tell him that I love him, and promise that I'll be back first thing in the morning. I update him on Gaby's new plans to deliver the baby in the hospital where he's located, and promise him that I'll inform him immediately if the baby comes during the night.

Returning home, I check on Gaby who is fast asleep in bed. I then write a quick e-mail to several of our closest friends to alert those who haven't heard about Bernie's heart attack:

December 23, 2008 11:00 p.m.

Dear Friends:

I wanted to let you know that Bernie had a serious heart attack today. He is in very critical but stable condition at Northlake Hospital. We are watching and waiting during the next twenty-four hours to see if his condition improves. They opened the blockage but he has apparently sustained some damage to his heart, which we will know more about tomorrow. Please pray for his complete recovery.

Love,

Judy

P.S. Gaby is in early labor and we are waiting for the baby to arrive at any moment. Please keep her in your prayers also.

I fall into bed hoping I'll be able to sleep with my anxiety brimming over about both Bernie and Gaby. I figure it's going to be a rough night, and I brace myself for more exhaustion tomorrow as I finally doze off. I can hardly believe Christmas is two days away.

Christmas Eve 2008

It's 4:30 a.m. and I awaken to the sound of the birthing party shuffling Gaby to the car to take her to the hospital. Apparently, her contractions have gotten so strong that she can't take the pain any longer, and Jo Jo wants to have her admitted to the hospital. Though they tried not to wake me, I want to go to the hospital with them. I throw on my clothes and grab my things for the short drive to the hospital. As the girls go through the admissions procedures in the Emergency Room, I head to the ICU to check on Bernie. Visiting hours begin at 5:00 a.m. and I count the minutes until I hear the loud click of the ICU doors, indicating that they are unlocked for entrance.

I'm relieved to see that Bernie appears to be stronger this morning and that he is looking much better. As I enter his ICU cubicle, the first words out of his mouth are "Judy, I have been praying 'The Memorare' all night and all I can see every time I close my eyes is the Immaculate Heart of Mary." The Memorare is a prayer that was written by St. Bernard in the Middle Ages imploring the Mother of Jesus for her help and intercession. Bernie loves it because his given name is Joseph Bernard, and he's taken to praying it daily these past few years.

Remember O most gracious Virgin Mary,
that never was it known that anyone who fled to your protection,
implored your help or sought your intercession was left unaided.
Inspired by this confidence, I fly unto Thee, O Virgin of Virgins,
my mother. To Thee I come, before Thee I stand, sinful and sorrowful.
O Mother of the Word Incarnate, despise not my petitions, but in Thy
Mercy, hear and answer me. Amen.

Bernie was raised Catholic, and though he has remained distant from God since I've known him, he has a devotion to the Blessed Mother. I attribute that to the fact that his alcoholic father, who died when Bernie was in his early twenties, made it difficult for him to perceive God as a kind, loving Father. His sweet Latin mother, on the other hand, managed to convey to her children a sense of warmth and love in spite of the problems in their home, and she has prayed a Rosary for her children every day of her life for more than fifty years.

My ninety-year-old mother-in-law Leticia, who stands all of four feet, ten inches tall and whom I dearly love, has one of those graphic, bloody crosses of Jesus' crucifixion in the bedroom of her Old Metairie home that are popular in Latin America. Though we Americans prefer to see Jesus presented neatly and cleanly on the Cross, the Latin American version of the Cross is probably more accurate, even though it is a little shocking at first blush. Their "bloody" Jesus seems to signify their acceptance of the scandal and violence of life, which "Letty" has known plenty of.

"God has been so wonderful to me," she says in her thick Columbian accent. "I have had a wonderful life." I've marveled at her perspective over the years, especially as I have heard the stories of her life.

"Henry was not married," she says matter-of-factly and without a grain of contempt for her husband. "I was married, but he was not." Bernie's father Henry was legendary for both his philandering and his alcohol consumption. Bernie, who grew up in an area of New Orleans called "Mid-City" from the time he was four, told me many times that his father would send him down to the neighborhood grocery store on Esplanade Avenue in the morning to buy a bottle of bourbon when he was just a little boy. Then the man would lie in bed listening to Edith Piaf all day, smoking and drinking as he lounged in his robe.

At night, when Henry was ready to go out, his dutiful wife would lay out the clothes she pressed for him so he could do "business" at the neighborhood bar. Letty, meanwhile, was taking English classes and working as a dental assistant to make ends meet. She would then knit baby booties all night long and send the children out to sell them to earn a few extra nickels. She eventually went to beauty school and became a hairdresser at John Jay Hair Salon, earning small-town fame as the TV hairdresser who styled noon news anchor Terry Fletrich's hair live on the local edition of the "Midday" show. Letty was also a legend at D.H. Holmes department store, where she worked at John Jay's in-store hair salon for years.

"God has been so good to me," she says often and convincingly in broken English. "I have never been alone because God has always been with me." I admire her faith and tenacity, because I know her life has not been easy. I cannot imagine coming to a foreign land with three young children to start life over in New Orleans without speaking a lick of English. Especially after moving from house to house in Bogota, Colombia, living off the kindness and sympathy of neighbors and friends while waiting for Henry to send for them, which I know she wondered at times if he really planned to do. "I would sit in the park all day with the children until sundown, praying that someone would invite us for dinner and to spend the night. And someone always did."

Yes, the bloody Jesus. He's the one for her.

As Bernie shares with me that he's seen the Immaculate Heart of Mary, I am relieved that we've apparently received a miracle and confident that Our Lady will intercede to save him. After kissing him goodbye, I race up to the Labor and Delivery Unit one floor above to see what's happening with Gaby. I meet Alex at the nurse's station and she informs me that Gaby has been put into a private room and that the doctor is expected shortly.

"God have mercy, Alex," I tell her. "I hope this doctor is not a quack. You never know who's going to be on call on Christmas Eve."

I've barely gotten those words out of my mouth when one of the most eccentric men I have ever seen literally sashays in front of us with large, round wave as he approaches the nurse's station.

"Lord help us, I hope that's not the doctor," I say in a panicky voice to Alex. Seconds later, the strange man comes up to us and introduces himself in a dramatic, theatrical voice.

"Hi, I'm Dr. Whiskey Houston and I'm on call," he says in a drawn out, nasal drawl as he extends a limp hand to greet us. "I'm going to go check on your daughter and I'll let you know how she's doing shortly." As he turns to enter Gaby's room, Alex and I stare at each other in complete disbelief.

"Who the hell names their child after a brand of alcohol?" Alex asks incredulously. "His parents must have been completely crazy!" she continues.

Minutes later, Dr. "Whiskey" emerges with a large smile on his face as he exits Gaby's room. With his index finger pointed in the air like John Travolta in "Saturday Night Live," he announces to us proudly as he sashays by again that he's "a water-popping Ninja!"

"God have mercy, Alex!" I say to her nervously again. "Gaby is going to be so upset! That is one of the weirdest doctors I have ever met!"

As I enter Gaby's room, she looks frightened and shaky. "The doctor ordered a Pitocin drip to speed up my contractions. I'm about four centimeters dilated and he wants to get this going so he can get home to his wife and children for Christmas Eve. He's ordering an epidural also."

"I'm so sorry, baby," I try to console her, knowing how much she had her heart set on her natural delivery with her midwives. "But the important thing is to get a healthy baby delivered. I know this is not what you planned, but let's just focus on getting the baby here." My heart breaks for her as I can see how much pain she is in. "You'll feel much better after you get the epidural," I promise her. "Your labor will be easy after that."

Once Gaby receives the epidural, she is calm and resting peacefully. I decide to go check on Bernie while Jo Jo, Kara and Alex sit with her. It's about 9:00 a.m. now and Grayson will be arriving at the hospital soon with nine-year-old Benjamin, with whom he stayed at home when we decided not to awaken Ben in the middle of the night. Grayson's family has just called, and they're on their way from South Carolina, hoping to arrive in time for the delivery.

I take the elevator down to the second floor ICU and find Dr. Madden next to Bernie's bed examining him. He has ordered another ultrasound and this time the news is very good. The ultrasound shows that Bernie's heart is beginning to regenerate and the doctor is thrilled. Bernie seems to have turned a corner and is heading in the right direction. It's Wednesday and Dr. Madden is hopeful that Bernie can go on home Friday if he continues to improve.

I spend the entire morning running back and forth between the ICU and the Labor and Delivery Unit. By noon, Grayson's parents, Bunny and Jay, have arrived at the hospital along with their two daughters Maggie, a senior at LSU, and Ginger, a junior in high school. My mother and both of my sisters have also gotten here, as well as Bernie's daughter Kerry, his daughter-in-law Lisa and his two granddaughters, Kaylie and Emily, who are thirteen and eleven respectively. Everyone stopped to see Bernie in the ICU first, and now more than a dozen people fill the waiting room in anticipation of James' birth. My mood has brightened considerably, and I'm only sorry that Bernie won't be up here with me to welcome our first grandson to the world. They've already told us that the baby isn't allowed in the ICU, so Bernie will have to wait until we get home to meet the little guy.

Around 12:30 I get a call while I'm in the ICU telling me to get upstairs right away, as Gaby is ready to deliver. I kiss Bernie's cheek and promise that I'll take plenty of pictures of Baby James. As I enter Gaby's room, the nurse tells me to scrub up and get ready.

The "water popping ninja" is now at the foot of Gaby's bed, instructing her to push. I'm standing beside her bed, and all I can hear is the old Helen Reddy song "I Am Woman" playing loudly in my head. Not "Amazing Grace." Not "How Great Thou Art." No. "I am woman, hear me roar…." I hear as I tell Gaby "Push, baby, push!" I momentarily reflect on the insanity of this situation, thinking "my husband's in critical condition, my son's in a rehab hospital, and I am standing next to my nineteen-year-old daughter trying to get a baby delivered on Christmas Eve!" This is almost too much, even for me. "Okay, God, I can do this if you help me," I pray. "Please help me!"

About thirty minutes later, James Gabriel enters the world, coming on Christmas Eve just like his godmother, Aunt Kara. I ooh and ahh over him for few minutes with Gaby and Grayson—marveling at the wonder of new life in this tiny baby's face—before we let the other family members, who are now anxiously waiting at the door, enter the room to see him.

"Congratulations, you two!" I say sincerely as I hug them in turn. "The baby is just beautiful."

After snapping plenty of pictures of James, who is the spitting image of his daddy, I take the camera and head back to the ICU to show Bernie pictures of our new grandbaby. When I get there, I am relieved to see that he is feeling stronger and we share our joy and pride over our precious little grandson. We also discuss the plan to depart the hospital with Gaby and James on Friday to head for home to rest and recuperate. It is a happy moment that is welcome reprieve from the last few days' events.

"That will work out perfectly," I tell him as I hold his hand and sit beside his bed with visible relief all over my face, feeling genuine hope for the first time that this may all turn out well after all. "You'll need a few weeks to recover from this at home," I continue. "Thank goodness it's Christmas and nobody is getting any work done. But you should be good as new by the New Year."

A short time later, I ride the elevator back up to the third floor and enter Gaby's room again, who now has uncontrollable shakes from the epidural. "That's the last time I will ever tell God how things are supposed to go down," she says sincerely, referring not only to her own aborted birthing plan, but to the many "imposed" medical interventions she clearly didn't want. "I know, baby," I tell her "I'm still trying to learn that I'm not in control. It's a hard lesson."

The rest of the day is actually happy, with the entire family cooing and rejoicing over our beautiful new baby boy for hours. Grayson and Alex assure me that they will help Gaby with the baby tonight, as the two of them are planning to spend the night in her hospital room. I arrive home in the dark after feeding Bernie his dinner, thankful to God that we have all survived the last forty-eight hours. I write a quick e-mail to my family and friends to update them on the situation.

Bernie Update: December 24, 2008 8:05 p.m.

Dear Friends:

Good news on all fronts. Bernie has improved miraculously today and the doctor says he should be able to leave the hospital by Friday. Frankly, it is a miracle he is alive and we are grateful to Our Lady for her presence with him. The first thing he told me this morning is the he "prayed the Memorare all night." Apparently she has her hand on him, thanks be to God. We are still waiting to hear exactly what damage he has to his heart, but he is strong as a horse and stubborn as a mule, which is a great help when one is sick.

Our daughter Gaby had a beautiful baby boy today at 1:30 p.m. James Gabriel weighed 7 lbs. 11 oz. and is healthy and peaceful. I ran between the second floor (ICU) and third floor (Labor and Delivery) all day, and thanks to a last minute change in Gaby's birthing plan, we were all able to be at the same hospital. James' grandparents and aunts managed to make it in from South Carolina before he arrived and the waiting room was full of loving, supportive family members. Daddy Grayson is beaming and the baby looks just like him. Pictures are forthcoming.

Thank you so much for your thoughts and prayers. God is good and we are grateful for every day we have to live, love and embrace life.

Have a blessed Christmas.
Love, Judy

Christmas Day 2008

7:00 a.m.

It's Christmas morning and I drag myself out of bed early to put out presents for Benjamin, who still believes in Santa Claus. We celebrate what is hands down the most depressing Christmas morning I have ever seen. I feign excitement as Benjamin finds his dirt bike, which he's thrilled about, then I haphazardly give some presents to Kara, whose birthday we skipped completely yesterday. Thankfully Bernie finished assembling the dirt bike right before he had the heart attack. I don't know what we would have done to salvage Christmas this year for Benjamin otherwise.

Benjamin, my fifth and Bernie's seventh child, came into our family when I was thirty-nine and Bernie was fifty-four. We'd had four children in four-and-a-half years before I turned thirty, and I, for one, was satisfied that "my quiver was full." Though I had come back to the Catholic Church in 1988, I still did not understand many of its teachings, including the one regarding contraception. Thinking that the celibate bishops who govern the Church couldn't possibly understand a thing about having a family, I boldly maintained that "I didn't want a bunch of old men at the Vatican telling me what to do with my sex life," and proceeded to get on the pill. After learning accidentally one day at a prayer meeting that the pill is an abortifacient, I was stopped dead in my tracks. I'll never forget how livid I was when I marched into my doctor's office for my next appointment, demanding that he tell me whether I'd been aborting my children unwittingly.

"You know how opposed to abortion I am!" I said with anguish in my voice as he, too, was Catholic and we had discussed the issue of abortion several times. "Do you mean to tell me I could have been aborting my children this entire time without even knowing it?" I demanded.

"Judy, that's not how the pill works," he insisted. "That's a fallacy." But the insert I had in my hand from the pill container betrayed his "facts." The first line of defense with birth control pills is to inhibit ovulation, the insert explained. But if breakthrough ovulation does occur, the second line of defense is to make the lining of the uterus inhospitable to human life, causing spontaneous abortion. As I relayed that information to him, I wondered how many other women who were against abortion were unaware of how the pill really works. Little did I know that conversation would be my first public defense of the Catholic Church's teaching on contraception, and that an opening had been created in my mind and heart that would cause the many objections I still had to the teaching of the Church, even as a practicing Catholic and daily communicant, to fall like dominos.

"I will never place myself under the authority of some man!" I had told a friend during a retreat at an old Carmelite monastery in the French Quarter one weekend as we discussed the authority of the Pope. "And I will NEVER confess my sins to a man. All I need is Jesus Christ and my Bible," I pontificated, spewing the party lines I had learned in non-denominational Protestantism right at her until she was reduced to tears. I had absolutely no idea at the time that Catholic bishops had written the parts of the Bible, and that the councils of the Catholic Church had ultimately decided in the fourth century which books the Bible would contain. It wasn't until some years later when I read former Presbyterian minister Scott Hahn's book "Rome Sweet Home" that I began to understand the history of the Church, and that the lines I was spewing were a rather modern invention that were incongruent with the way the Church had operated through most of history.

Though I had thought very little about it, I had sort of imagined that the Bible had magically "fallen" out of the sky at some point in Church history, and I just assumed everyone had access to the Bible throughout the history of the Church. It never occurred to me that Bibles were rare and incredibly expensive before the Sixteenth Century advent of the printing press due to the fact Catholic monks had to laboriously copy them by hand, or that most people were illiterate until the early Twentieth Century. I mean, for crying out loud, my own grandmother had only an eighth-grade education and Bernie's mother had less education than that!

"Duh! Where has my brain been?" I asked myself after the light finally came on and I became convinced that the whole "Bible alone" mantra is not only unbiblical, it's positively illogical. "To be deep in history is to cease to be Protestant," Blessed John Henry Newman famously said after his conversion to Catholicism. "To be deep in Western history is to cease to be anti-Catholic," I like to add. At least that was true for me.

"Learn and defend the Catholic faith!!!" I had clearly heard God say to me in an inaudible voice that shook me from my head to my toes as I closed the pages of "Rome Sweet Home." And though no one was more surprised than me when I was called by God to study Catholic theology, God knew that it would fit me like a glove and I've loved teaching

Apologetics, Catholic Sexual Ethics and Bioethics ever since. Needless to say, I'm now completely convinced that the Church actually "gets it" about everything concerning faith and morals, even though I have a lively awareness that sinners like me constantly sully her reputation.

When the Church's teaching finally grabbed hold of me, Bernie was generous enough to agree to practice Natural Family Planning, and we surrendered our contraceptives cold turkey. Four years later Benjamin Joseph Klein was born. All the doctor could say as a hall full of fifteen people cheered loudly at Bernie's announcement of the baby's arrival was "I've never seen a family so happy about the birth of a fifth child!" Though the doctor was genuinely perplexed at the strong reaction to this child's birth, we were all thrilled. Not surprisingly, giving up our contraceptives had removed the barrier in our hearts and minds about having more children. And though I had been terrified about having another child while I was contracepting, I eventually became open to the possibility as God changed my heart over time.

The lagniappe came in the form of Benjamin's white hair and blue eyes, and the moment I saw him I announced that the German genes had finally kicked in. Though Bernie's Latin genes had dominated our first four children's looks, I now held a white haired, blue-eyed baby that looked exactly like me in my arms, and he was living proof to me that God can continually expand our capacity for love.

"Love multiplies, it doesn't divide," my mother always said when I voiced my fears about whether I had enough love in me to adequately meet the needs of yet another child. And boy, was she right. Benjamin's feet never hit the ground for the first two years of his life and I literally had to fight the kids to hold him. It was a very happy time for all of us, and we continually joke that Benjamin has been "well loved." I thank God for that as I watch him run gleefully into the street to ride his dirt bike, thinking he's going to need all the love he can get right now.

Christmas Day

8:30 a.m.

I hurry off to the hospital to see Bernie and, alarmingly, I find him distressed and in a visibly weakened condition. He refuses to open the Christmas presents I've brought for him, and instructs me to put them on the table next to the bed instead.

"Judy," he says as I enter his cubicle. "I prayed 'The Memorare' all night and I see the Immaculate Heart of Mary every time I close my eyes. Baby," he continues soberly, "I can feel my organs shutting down and I know I'm going to die."

"What?!!!" I respond forcefully. "You are not going to die!" I assert even more vigorously. I must admit that there were times in our marriage when I would have welcomed an exit from our relationship, but staring the possibility of Bernie's death straight in the face has jolted me into a panic over the reality that he might, indeed, die. That thought has sent me into the "fight or flight" mode, and the fight has arisen within me that conveys with intensity that I am prepared to defend Bernie's life like a mother tiger shielding her cubs from a predator.

"The doctor said you're doing much better and you'll be home by Friday!" I insist.

"No, Judy," he continues with resignation and not at all like the Bernie I have known who has fought every battle of his life with a vengeance. "I'm dying. I can feel it," he states flatly.

Shortly thereafter, Dr. Madden enters the room followed by the ultrasound machine and technician. As the technician squirts the gooey jelly around Bernie's chest, I can feel my anxiety starting to rise. The ultrasound confirms Bernie's self-diagnosis and Dr. Madden sighs deeply before speaking.

"This is exactly what I had hoped would not happen," he shares with obvious concern and disappointment in his voice. "He's gone into cardiogenic shock and is in congestive heart failure." This new description of Bernie's condition—congestive heart failure—falls like a crushing blow on both of us and Bernie looks at me for the first time since his heart attack with real fear on his face.

56

"What are we going to do?" I ask the doctor blankly.

"Well, I think the best option at the moment is to put a balloon pump on him to assist his heart in beating. That should help his heart rest so he can hopefully begin to recover," the doctor says with a worried look on his face. "We can do the surgery right away, but I need you to sign the consent forms so we can proceed."

After signing all of the forms, I head upstairs to check on Gaby and James and to give the kids the news while they prep Bernie for surgery. As I exit the elevator, I find Grayson's parents, Bunny and Jay, standing in the hall. Though I try my best to maintain my composure, I can't stop myself from breaking down and sobbing.

"What is wrong?" Bunny asks in her usual sweet voice, which is a raspy mix of Lafayette Cajun and South Carolina drawl.

"Bernie's in congestive heart failure and the doctor needs to put a balloon pump in his heart to help it beat," I cry. "Bernie told me he thinks he's dying and I am so worried!"

"Oh, honey," she says as she wraps her arms around me with tears in her eyes. "Bernie's been so wonderful to Gaby and Grayson through this whole ordeal. He's just GOT to get home so he can hold that sweet baby! Listen," she continues, "don't you worry about a thing. You stay down there with Bernie and we'll stay here and help Gaby."

Bunny and I have hit it off since the first time we spoke on the phone several months ago in June, after she and Jay got the news about the pregnancy and called from South Carolina to introduce themselves. I'd felt much better about her after learning that she grew up in Lafayette and went to LSU, and her strong connection to Louisiana had come as a huge relief to me. Family ties run very deep in Louisiana, and practically everyone here is related. If they're not related, they're sure to know your family and friends. Bunny and I figured out during our first phone conversation that a dear friend of mine from high school was her roommate in college, as well as the fact that we know several of the same Louisianans from Jackson Hole, Wyoming, where members of both of our families own homes. We'd made plans to meet at our home for dinner over Labor Day weekend when she and Jay would be in Louisiana for an LSU football game. And we'd both agreed that lots of wine would make the meeting much easier on all of us.

Bunny and I have spoken on the phone many times since then and she'd even flown in for Gaby's baby shower last month. I never cease to be amazed that, though we were total strangers just three months ago, we're sharing grand parenting duties today. I tell everyone about wonderful Bunny and Jay, and I can honestly say that I'm grateful they have landed in our laps.

I dry my tears and gather my courage to enter Gaby's room. I don't want to scare her, as she's already carrying so much weight on her young shoulders. I share selected pieces of the news about Bernie with Gaby and Alex, who are huddled in bed trying to get some rest after a sleepless night, while Grayson is passed out cold in a chair in the corner of the room. I hold James for a few minutes and kiss his tiny, tender face repeatedly, thanking God for the gift of his life. Trying to downplay the seriousness of the situation, I assure the girls their Dad will be okay. I then head down to the ICU and sit in the waiting room crying as I phone my sister Renee, the nurse, to get her assessment of Bernie's medical condition. It is obvious by the sleeping bags, pillows and other equipment in the waiting room that some patients' family members have been here a very long time. "God have mercy," I pray as I think of that prospect. "Please let Bernie get well."

The surgery goes well and Bernie is returned to his cubicle, now accompanied by the ever-present thumping of the balloon pump, thrusting blood to his heart. After a long, emotional day and many visits to the third floor to see the baby, I finally head home to get some sleep. Tomorrow is Friday and it doesn't look like Bernie will be coming home any time soon. I arrange for Jo Jo to bring Gaby home from the hospital in the morning, then to stay at our house to hold down the fort in my absence. I'm beginning to realize that I may be at the hospital for some time. I've never had such a strange, dreadful Christmas. I'm so grateful for my siblings and for the fact that I can always depend on them. And I'm grateful the hospital is only ten minutes away from home.

December 26, 2008

I arrive at the hospital very early in the morning and Dr. Madden is already there, assessing Bernie's condition. With a very serious face, he tells me that Bernie's lungs are beginning to fill with fluid and that he's probably developed an infection, as he spiked a fever during the night.

"His breathing is labored and I'd like to put him on a ventilator so he can rest while the machine breathes for him," the doctor says. "But I need your permission to give him a paralyzing agent that will keep his body completely still so he won't try to pull the tube out of his throat." I have the feeling he's choosing his words very carefully so as not to alarm me, and I barely whisper "of course." I remember when we got the news that Marshall had to be "intubated," and it was a very bad sign. Once again, I sign the necessary consent forms and standing beside Bernie, I lay my hands on him and begin to pray.

"Please Jesus, let my husband recover," I ask silently and sincerely. Feeling overwhelmed with regret at how unsympathetic I've been about the amount of stress he's been carrying these past few years, I implore God for another chance. "Please, Lord," I continue "just let my husband come home with me. I'll be much more appreciative of him this time." I kiss Bernie's face again and tell him I love him as they wheel him out into the hall for the surgery. As I walk beside his stretcher going toward the operating room, he looks up with a pitiful expression and begs me to let him see the baby.

"Honey, I'm so sorry, they won't let us bring the baby into the ICU," I say with my voice cracking as I walk beside him holding his hand. "Please get well so you can come home with us."

The nurses return Bernie to the ICU within the hour and he's now in a drug-induced coma. He's received the Sacrament of the Sick three times since his heart attack, and several priest friends are ready-at-hand to come to the hospital to administer it again if he takes a turn for the worst. In the sacrament, which used to be called Last Rites, the priest anoints the sick person's forehead and hands with oil, asking the Lord to heal them. It is mentioned in James 5:14-15, which says: "Is any among you sick? Let him call for the elders of the church, and let them pray over him, anointing him with oil in the name of the Lord; and the prayer of faith will save the sick man, and the Lord will raise him up; and if he has committed sins, he will be forgiven."

Alex, Gaby, Grayson and James leave the hospital around noon. My panic shoots up a notch as my family departs the facility, and I face the sinking feeling that I'm now in this alone. I call several doctor friends throughout the day to get their opinions about Bernie's condition as I sit in that God-forsaken waiting room with my own blankets and pillows, crying nonstop. No one is very reassuring and Bernie's general physician tells me to "prepare myself." Though I do not allow myself to believe for a minute that my husband is going to die, I am worried that Christian, who is still in a rehab facility in Tennessee, will never forgive me if Bernie should pass away without him being here to say goodbye. "Maybe I should bring Christian home from rehab," I tell several friends. "But I'm so worried he may relapse from the stress."

Early in the afternoon, I go home temporarily to check on Gaby, James and the kids. As I drive down my street, my neighbor, who is a neurosurgeon at the hospital and who's heard about the condition Bernie's in, stops me. After giving him an update on the morning's happenings, I share my concern about whether I should bring Christian back from Tennessee to see his father, given the delicate nature of Christian's recovery.

"It sounds like it's time for you to bring your son home to say goodbye to his father," he says solemnly. "I would suggest you bring your son home right away," he continues with more urgency.

With that, I get on the phone and arrange for Christian to fly into New Orleans as soon as possible, booking him on the first available flight in the morning. I then sit at my desk long enough to send out a quick e-mail to a growing list of family and friends on the "Bernie Update" e-mail list to implore their prayers.

Bernie Update: Sat, 26 Dec 2008 1:42 p.m.
Subject: Prayers Needed

Dear Friends:

For those who have not heard, my husband Bernie Klein suffered a massive heart attack on Dec. 23. He is in stable but very critical condition at the moment, and we are in dire need of prayer for his recovery. We are asking everyone we know to pray that his heart resumes normal function and that his blood pressure comes up. Also please pray for protection against infections.

Many thanks and God bless.

Judy

Then I head back to the hospital to stay with Bernie until visiting hours end at 10:00 p.m. I'm tired and terrified, but there's nothing else to do but sit beside him and pray when they allow me into his room every few hours to see him. Between visits, I call home to check on the kids or sit in the waiting room trying to field the many phone calls coming in from family and friends. People have begun to show up at the hospital to keep me company, as the word has hit the street that Bernie is very critical. Meals have also started arriving at the house, brought by many well-wishers who know that there are only two things to do in a life-threatening crisis: eat and pray.

By late evening, I'm back at home holding sweet baby James until I finally fall into bed completely exhausted. It feels like I have just fallen asleep when the phone rings at 3:00 a.m. It's the male nurse from the hospital on the line telling me to come immediately because Bernie is failing. I arouse all of the children, including Benjamin, and we head to the hospital in haste. I also call Fr. John from Our Lady of the Lake Church to come anoint him again. I then call Bernie's sister Hedy, who has lived three hours away in Natchez, Mississippi since Hurricane Katrina. I tell her she should come to the hospital—right away.

December 27, 2008

3:30 a.m.

The kids and I enter Bernie's ICU cell and he appears to be sleeping peacefully. The nurse informs us that the oxygen level in his blood fell to 70% several hours ago, which is a clear sign that his body is shutting down. The girls and I gather around his bed and begin to pray a Rosary, and their voices bring the nurse to tears as they sing the "Ave" in between the decades, just the way Aunt Hedy taught them.

Fr. John has been called and he arrives quickly from Our Lady of the Lake Church to anoint Bernie for a fourth time. I'm wondering if we're abusing the Sacrament of the Sick at this point, but God knows we're desperate. Hedy gets to the hospital around 6:30 a.m. with several of her daughters, and I watch somberly as she says a heart-wrenching goodbye to her big brother thinking, of course, that she'll never see him again. The nurses change shifts at seven a.m., and we sit with Bernie throughout the morning observing that there is no change in his condition.

Several hours into the vigil, the new nurse on duty informs us that the dying process will probably take days and he suggests that we go home to take a break and get some rest. Bernie's blood oxygen level has even improved slightly since we arrived, so we decide to go to my house to regroup. "Nurse," I instruct as I walk out of the ICU, "please call me immediately if Mr. Klein gets into a crisis."

"Lady," he replies looking at me as though I'm completely crazy "he is IN a crisis."

"Right, right," I say haltingly, embarrassed at my seeming stupidity. "Call me if he gets into a BIGGER crisis."

Though I now feel even more ridiculous with the second stupid statement, the nurse just replies, "Will do," as we exit the ICU.

Coming into our home, Hedy and her girls take turns holding James and we marvel at the timing of this new baby coming into our family the moment we appear to be losing Bernie. We also share our amazement at the "God-incident" of all of us having had an impromptu two night slumber party here just this past weekend in honor of my mother-in-law's ninetieth birthday. Everyone had been in an unusually jovial mood and we squeezed five extra people into the beds upstairs as we ate, visited and shared about the goings on in our lives. Bernie had been especially happy to have his sister and nieces here for several days, which was unusual for a man who was easily bored with company, and who flipped the lights on and off when he decided it was time for people to depart, imitating his own father's ritual when he was ready for the guests to leave. How ironic that they would all sleep at our home for the first time in twenty-four years, and bid Bernie goodbye the day before he would have a massive heart attack!

I call the hospital to check on Bernie and decide that I'd better get back to the ICU, even though the nurse confirms that he's stable. Christian has landed at the airport, and a friend offers to pick him up and bring him to the hospital. I'm nervous about seeing him for the first time since Family Weekend in Tennessee two weeks ago, and am worried about how he's going to react to the situation here.

I arrive at the hospital to find my sister Renee, who has come to check on Bernie and help translate all of the medical jargon for me. Renee, who is four years older than me, worked for years as a nurse before she became a licensed contractor with her own construction company. She is the third child and eldest daughter in our family of ten children and she's always taken a leadership role in the family, especially in medical matters. We still rib her about the fact that, though she was nearly the same age as the rest of us, she was given the authority to punish and spank us if necessary, as she was often left in charge while our mother went to the grocery or to run errands. One day, it suddenly dawned on the other nine of us in her care that Renee was really of our generation, even though she acted so much older. Upon that realization, we threw down the gauntlet against her authority and refused to obey her ever again.

Though it was a mutiny from which she would never recover, she still holds a position of power over the rest of us in life matters, and to this day, she still tries to tell me what to do. At this moment, I NEED her to tell me what to do, as I am way in over my head in this hospital with a critically ill husband to make decisions for. Renee assures me we've taken the right course of action for Bernie thus far, and she's still hopeful that he can recover from this trauma. I take great solace in her words and in her confident presence, and I thank God for my two sisters Renee and Jo Jo, who have never failed me when I need them.

Christian finally arrives. He is stunned and devastated to see just how sick his father really is and sobs helplessly beside Bernie's bed. I can smell the alcohol on his breath and my heart breaks as I realize that he's already relapsed, numbing himself to come and face this scene. "I can't deal with that right now," I tell myself as I try to gather my courage for what lies ahead. "I have to focus completely on Bernie right now."

Bernie improves steadily throughout the day, thank God, and eventually we head back to the house to try to get some rest, instructing the hospital staff to call immediately if there's any change in his condition. Arriving home, I send a quick update to the growing list of prayer warriors who are beseeching heaven for Bernie's healing before I collapse into bed hoping to get some much needed sleep.

Bernie Update: December 27, 2008

Dear Friends:

After being called to the hospital at 3:00 a.m. because Bernie was in serious distress, I am relieved to report that he has managed to improve today. Apparently his heart is still in shock and the doctors are trying to give his body as much rest as possible by using a ventilator to help him breathe and a balloon pump to assist his heart in beating. He is under sedation, but is responsive when the sedation is lightened and he appears to be neurologically sound.

He has been anointed four times we are asking the Lord to heal him completely. Right now are waiting and praying from hour to hour, but we are still hopeful that his heart can begin to do its job again. The main things we need prayer for are protection from complications and infections and that his heart will recover from shock.

We are so grateful for all of the love and support we have received from all around the world. We have many loving family members helping us and we have been much consoled by the presence of my sister Renee, who is a nurse (translating all of the medical stuff for me) and my sister Joanne, who is an incredibly giving person and is holding down the fort for me at home.

Keep the prayers coming.

Blessings.

Judy

December 28, 2008

7:00 a.m.

I awaken to a phone call from Dr. Madden, telling me he has good news. "Bernie's fever broke during the night and he appears to be doing better," he conveys in an optimistic voice. "Ochsner has agreed to take him and put him on the heart transplant waiting list. It's his only hope of survival now. They're sending an ambulance to pick him up."

"Wow," I respond, thinking how odd it is that being on a heart transplant list suddenly sounds like good news. "Is the ambulance on its way?"

"Not yet. You need to come right away to sign all of the papers for his release. The ambulance will be here sometime this morning," Madden continues. With that, the game plan changes, and I quickly dress and head to the hospital to sign discharge papers for Bernie's release to Ochsner Medical Center, a renowned trauma center in New Orleans that specializes in heart transplantation surgery.

At the hospital, I meet with the various specialists who are now treating Bernie, and sign a stack of papers giving permission for him to be transferred to another facility. "The ambulance is on its way," Dr. Madden alerts me. "You can either ride in it with Bernie or follow in your own car." I decide that it's best to take my own car, and suddenly realize that I need to go home to pack a suitcase, as the hospital is forty-five minutes away and running to and from home base will no longer be an option. I inform the doctor that I'm going to get my things, and that I'll be back within thirty minutes to meet the ambulance, asking him not to let them leave without me. Meanwhile, I call my daughter Kara to tell her to pack and come with me as I race home and run into the house.

I enter through the garage and pass Grayson and a group of his fraternity brothers sitting on the sofa outside my bedroom talking and laughing, as they have come to see the baby for the first time. I make my

66

way into my bedroom and am intercepted by Christian, who closes the door behind us to inform me that he's not going back to rehab.

"I'm not discussing that right now, Christian," I utter as I hastily move toward my closet to gather the clothes I'll need to stay in New Orleans. "I've got to get to the hospital right away to meet the ambulance."

"But, Mom," he continues anyway, "I need to talk to you right now about my plans."

"Christian, I'm in a hurry." I say more aggressively, feeling the pressure within me building like a teakettle that's about to blow, "I'm not discussing that right now!!"

"You never have time to discuss anything with me!" he counters insistently. "I need to talk to you about rehab!!!"

"CHRISTIAN, I AM NOT TALKING ABOUT THAT RIGHT NOW!!" I screech in drawn-out words at the top of my lungs with such volume and intensity that it jolts even me. In the face of that unbridled display of emotion, he backs away from me and exits the bedroom. I follow right behind him with suitcase in hand, only to realize that Grayson and his friends are sitting on the sofa just feet from my bedroom, and there's no way they could have missed that maniacal display seconds ago.

"Hi, guys," I say in the most pleasant voice I can muster, faking a smile as I speak. "How are ya'll doing?" Their poker faces do not betray that they overheard me screaming at Christian, but I am mortified nonetheless. "Yes, I am completely crazy," I say under my breath as I walk to the car with Kara, explaining to her what just happened.

"Don't worry about it, Mom," she says in a sweet, reassuring voice. "Surely they understand how much pressure you're under." But the voice in my head that's full of blame and regret is not so kind, and it beats me up all the way to the hospital.

The ambulance finally arrives and Kara and I follow the EMTs outside, where they proceed to spend an hour trying to figure out how to fit Bernie's stretcher and all of his equipment into the ambulance.

"Seriously, guys, you have to be kidding," I say as I watch them repeatedly rearrange Bernie, the IV bags, the balloon pump and the ventilator trying to get them all into the too-small space. After a good hour of arranging and rearranging, they finally slam the doors shut and race off toward the South shore, with Kara and I following right behind. "Note to self," I tell Kara, "when Dad gets well, we're going to start a business that designs and builds ambulances that can actually hold all of equipment of a critically ill patient. I've never seen anything so ridiculous in my life!"

We follow the ambulance onto the Causeway, and though I'm trying my best to keep up, it's impossible due to the fact that the driver is going at least 110 MPH. "Why in the hell is he going so fast?" I ask Kara, obviously hiding myself in denial about how acute Bernie's condition really is. We watch helplessly as the vehicle disappears from sight, then we pray a Rosary not only for Bernie's recovery, but that we can find him when we get to Ochsner, which is a massive medical complex that covers several city blocks.

We arrive at the hospital around 1:00 p.m. and the two of us wander around anxiously for at least a half an hour trying to figure out where Bernie is. Renee has met the ambulance there, and she finally calls my cell phone to instruct us to come to the Cardiac Intensive Care Unit on the eighth floor to meet her while the doctor assesses Bernie. Meanwhile, Alex and Christian arrive.

After what seems like an eternity, Dr. Brit Meiser, a fifty-ish looking cardiologist, comes into the waiting room at 10:00 p.m. and asks if he can speak to me privately. "Oh my God," I whisper to Renee "this can't be good if he wants to speak to me alone." Especially since we're the only ones in the waiting room, which at this point has become completely dark and empty.

Meiser leads Renee and me into the Family Conference Room in the corner, where we sit and brace ourselves for what he is about to say.

"Mrs. Klein, did they tell you at Northlake that your husband is in total organ failure?" he begins.

"No they did not," I reply, confused as to why Dr. Madden told me he was doing better.

"Well, his heart has failed, his liver has failed, his kidneys have failed and his lungs have failed," he continues pointedly, "and we don't know if he has any brain function. Though we're going to do everything we can do to save him, there's less than a ten percent chance he'll make it through the night. I suggest that you and your children stay by his side tonight."

"What???" I respond in total disbelief, feeling my denial crumbling around me like a dilapidated brick wall. "How can that be possible? They told us he was doing better and that they were sending him here for a heart transplant!"

"I'm sorry, Mrs. Klein, your husband's not a candidate for a heart transplant. You have to be strong enough to undergo the surgery, and he's just too sick. My best guess is that he won't survive the night. You and your children can come into his room now and sit with him," he offers as he shakes my hand pointedly and leaves the room.

My protective sister assures me as I fall apart crying that that was "too rough" a delivery of information, and that doctors can't always predict what's going to happen to a patient. "That's right," I respond as I do my best to gather myself together, trying to find hope somehow. "In any case, if he's going to die tonight, at least we will be with him holding his hand and praying," I say, finding some consolation in that thought.

The children and I enter Bernie's room to find that two nurses have set up stations at the foot of his bed and attached at least twenty bags of IV drips to his body, which hang around his bed connected to high tech monitors that titrate his medication every few seconds in an attempt to keep him alive. A dialysis machine has been added to the balloon pump and ventilator, and the room is so full of equipment that it's hard to find a space to stand up, much less sit by him. The nurse pulls a chair beside Bernie's bed for me, and the girls squeeze around his bed as we proceed to pray the Rosary, the Divine Mercy and Prayers for the Dying. Christian, who cannot bear seeing his father in this condition, curls up in the easy chair in the corner with his eyes closed tight, refusing to see any of this. Finding a Gideon's Bible in a drawer in the corner, we proceed to pray the Psalms aloud; along with other Scripture verses that we hope Bernie can hear to give him courage and peace. The hospital chaplain is called to anoint him again, and the vigil continues for several hours as we lift our voices in unison, and as the girls sing in harmony beside Bernie to comfort him on what, one more time, we believe will be his last night on earth.

December 29, 2008

2:00 a.m.

Our deathwatch is interrupted when the male nurse asks us to go into the waiting room so he can shock Bernie's heart to correct its erratic rhythm, but not before I sign more consent forms that say that I understand that this intervention can give him brain damage or a stroke.

"God have mercy," I say, as we sit like ghosts in the dark, cold waiting room again. "This is just too horrible to be believed." About twenty minutes later, we hear an alarm go off and all I can hear is the sound of a nurse over the CICU speaker announcing, "Code blue! Code blue!" I spontaneously jump from my seat and try to run through the CICU doors to be with my husband, only to find them locked tight with no one in sight to open them.

"Damn it!!" I scream as I frantically bang on the locked doors trying to get someone's attention, morphing into Aurora in the hospital scene in "Terms of Endearment." "I didn't tell the nurse that I want to be with him when he dies! I need to get in there!! Open the doors!!!" I shout at the top of my lungs in desperation as I repeatedly slam my fists on the glass doors with all of my might. Getting no response, I run up and down the halls around the waiting room trying to find someone—anyone—to let me in. Finally, I locate a nurse working in an office and scream that my husband is dying and that I need to get into his room.

"What's your nurse's name?" she asks as she walks with me back through the waiting room.

"I have no idea," I say blankly. "He's that nice looking black nurse with the green eyes," is the only description I can think of.

"Mom!!!!" my children react together, embarrassed by my politically incorrect terminology. "He's not black!!!"

71

"Right, I mean, I mean...he's Creole!" is all I can respond, which just makes them sink deeper into their seats.

The nurse disappears through the CICU doors and reappears within minutes, telling me that the "Code Blue" was not for my husband, and that our nurse will come get me as soon as he gets Bernie settled. My adrenaline is racing to the point that I feel like I'm going to have a panic attack, and I try to breathe to calm myself down. Five minutes later, our nurse comes to gather us back into Bernie's room, and our vigil of prayer continues until he asks us to leave the room again so he can shock Bernie's heart.

"Look," I say, not taking any chances this time, "if he dies I want to be in here with him. Send someone to get me if he is dying!! It's really important to me to be with him when he goes." The nurse assures me he will send for me if necessary, and off we go again to the dark, freezing cold waiting room where we huddle together, trembling in terror.

Around 2:30 a.m., the nurse calls us to the back again, where we pray out loud for another hour. The children are beginning to fade and so am I, so Kara and I lie together on the small, built-in sofa under the window while Christian sleeps in the corner recliner, and Alex lies with a blanket and pillow on the ice-cold concrete floor. Within minutes, the "Creole" nurse instructs us to cover our ears as he has to shock Bernie's heart a third time, and there's no time for us to leave the room. I cover my ears and try to pray as I hear the loud "Whap! Whap! Whap!" of the defibrillator sending electricity to Bernie's heart in an attempt to keep it beating. The entire scene is surreal and terrifying, and I literally feel like I'm going to shake out of my skin. Kara and I are huddling together under a blanket as my body rattles uncontrollably, and I'm embarrassed that my fear is so transparent to her.

The nurse finally gets Bernie's heart to establish a normal rhythm again, and I look up at the clock and notice that it's four a.m. I'm exhausted beyond description and need to doze off for five minutes to recharge my brain. "Please Lord," I pray as I close my eyes. "Wake me up in five minutes. And please don't let Bernie die while I'm asleep."

No sooner have I closed my eyes than I experience my spirit leaving my body. Nothing like this has ever remotely happened to me before, but I can clearly see myself floating around the room looking down until I stop at Bernie's bedside. I am watching myself as I stand beside my husband yelling insistently to him "Fight, Bernie!!! You have to fight!!! Do not give up!!! Fight!!!" I can distinctly see and hear myself from a distance, and somehow I know that I am still on the sofa *and* I am standing next to Bernie's bed imploring him not to give up.

A second later, I'm back in my body wide awake and the first thought that enters my mind is "I don't know what just happened, but I know that was real. That really happened."

It occurs to me immediately that it has something to do with St. Pio of Pietrelcina, a Twentieth Century priest, who was the first priest in the history of the Church to bear the "stigmata" or wounds of Christ on his body. The old Franciscan friar was known for his gift of bi-location, and stories abound about him appearing to the dying to heal them while he was still alive and living in San Giovanni Rotondo in Italy, where his incorrupt body now lies.

My dry cleaner, who brought me a relic of the saint one day while delivering our clothing, had introduced me to Padre Pio many years ago. Because Bernie and Padre Pio shared the same May 25 birthday, I felt that he could be a special intercessor for my husband, and proceeded to put the relic under Bernie's side of the mattress, hoping and praying that Pio's strong intercession before God would heal the wounds in Bernie's mind and heart that kept him from embracing God as a loving, merciful Father. I have prayed to the saint for Bernie ever since then, and even made a pilgrimage to his shrine six months ago in June to have masses said for my husband's healing and conversion.

The catalyst for that pilgrimage had been a visit I'd made in May 2007 to an exorcist in New Orleans—just a few months after my brother Stephen and his wife Brenda's murder-suicide.

At that time, I had called Fr. Michael Bendsome to have some intergenerational healing masses said for my family of origin. He and I had met three times to discuss the Landrieu family history in order to discern the spiritual root of the suicides and murder now present in our family. I shared with Fr. Bendsome the tragic story of my own father, who had accidentally shot and almost killed his little brother, Moon, as he fired a shotgun when my father was seven and his brother was just three.

My father had then developed an obsession with guns that would last throughout his life, and much of his spare time while we were growing up had been spent loading shotgun shells in the basement of our home. He'd eventually become a gun dealer with an extensive gun collection, and that my brothers would both shoot themselves with guns given to them by my father was the frightful family-legacy coda for which I was seeking healing prayer. I conveyed our sad history to the exorcist, as well as my personal belief that much of the violence in our family was somehow connected to the trauma my father sustained when he shot his baby brother. We talked extensively about my father and brothers and about my concern for my son, Christian; whom I feared might be next to die.

During all three meetings with Fr. Bendsome I never spoke about Bernie at all, as I was totally focused on my own bloodline, specifically on my brothers and son. But as I got up to leave Father's office the last time we met, he opened the door of his office to let me out in to the hall. Before I could leave he closed the door again, then turned and looked me right in the eye and asked a most peculiar question.

"Does your husband like baseball bats?" he asked inquisitively in his soft-spoken Irish brogue.

"No, I don't think so…why?" I hesitated, wondering why he would ask me such an odd question.

"Because he's getting ready to get hit by an enormous one by God," he continued gently.

"What does that mean?" I replied, feeling the blood drain from my body, knowing that prophecy couldn't be good.

"I don't have time to tell you that right now, but I'll tell you the next time you come back," was all he gave in response.

With that, Fr. Bendsome turned and hurried out of the room and never answered a phone call or e-mail from me again. Sensing for months that something terrible was getting ready to happen to Bernie, I finally began a thirty-one-day novena for him—a novena being the recitation of prayers for a special purpose during a specified number of consecutive days with the hope of obtaining a miracle through the grace of God. The novena was to St. Joseph, as Bernie's given name was Joseph Bernard, and because St. Joseph is the patron saint of fathers and families. And though I didn't plan it this way, I would wind up concluding my St. Joseph Novena for Bernie at St. Pio's shrine in Italy just six months ago in June, when I arrived in Rome on Father's Day weekend for a week of bioethics classes.

As God would have it, I had landed in Rome the day before Father's Day on June 15, 2008. I was hell-bent on getting to St. Pio's Shrine in San Giovanni Rotondo to pray for Bernie and to see the saint's newly exhumed, perfectly incorrupt body and I convinced my girlfriend Kiron, who happens to be a tour guide in Italy, to come with me. We took the three-hour train ride to the little mountainside village that is laden with ancient olive tree groves, some of them over a thousand years old. We then spent Father's Day at St. Pio's shrine, where they were having a special celebration in honor of his canonization. It was a total God-incidence that Father's Day happened to be the thirty-first day of my novena to St. Joseph —as well as the very day St. Pio was canonized seven years earlier! The convergence of dates struck me deeply and I sensed that God was doing something very powerful—even though I could not fully understand what it was at the time.

I lie here now on this surreal night six months later thinking about that uncanny intersection of events, wondering what in the world I just experienced with that out-of-body event. I conclude that St. Pio must be praying for Bernie and for me, and I also have a hunch that I was

75

interceding for Bernie as he was actually dying. Whatever the case may be, Bernie miraculously makes it through the night, and the kids and I are sleeping peacefully when the nurse awakens us at 6:45 a.m. to inform us we need to leave the room for shift change.

The doctors arrive soon thereafter for morning rounds and one advises us that Bernie is "the sickest patient in Louisiana." Though it's a dubious honor no one would want to have, I'm just happy he's still alive. His blood pressure is far below the level needed to sustain life, so they are giving him bags of "pressers" or medications that pull the blood from the extremities and "press" it toward the heart, making his hands and feet turn blue and his fingers black. The rest of his body has turned yellow from liver failure, and to see him in this condition is excruciatingly painful.

Because of the voluminous number of medical personnel that are coming in and out of the room, including at least fifteen different teams of specialists, the two nurses stationed at the foot of his bed, and all of the supporting personnel needed to deal with his equipment, the nurses instruct me that everyone else must leave the room except me, and that I must stay out of the way so they can access the patient. I've never seen such a fast-paced, intense working environment in my life and the stress level stays at a fever pitch all day long in his room. Kara and Alex stay at the hospital with me, even though they have to wait outside the room. Bernie's daughter Kerry is also here with us, wanting to keep watch over her father as he did for her a dozen years ago during her own hospital stay. Christian, who can't handle the tension here, heads home to wait the crisis out. Meanwhile, Jo Jo is still there helping Gaby and Grayson with the baby and taking care of Benjamin as well.

Most of the day I sit in the chair in the corner trying to pray, but I'm so exhausted that the best I can do is close my eyes and picture myself climbing up the Cross with Jesus, putting my arms around His neck and holding on for dear life. It feels like our lives have been suspended in mid-air as I sit beside my dying husband for the seventh straight day, thinking how strange it is that people are marching on with their lives all around us, seemingly oblivious to the life altering tragedies like ours that are occurring constantly in their midst.

We manage to end the day with Bernie somewhat more stable, and the nurses advise me that I should try to get some rest at the hotel that's attached to the hospital, as sleeping will be impossible in the hospital room with the continuous clanging of the alarms on the equipment indicating that a medication or a machine needs to be adjusted immediately. Though it seems too far away for comfort, my sister Renee books me a room in the hotel adjoining the building, and I ambivalently make my way through the block-long, pitch-dark corridor that leads from the hospital to the hotel to meet Kara and Alex and hopefully grab a few hours of sleep.

December 31, 2008

It's New Year's Eve and Bernie has made it through another two days with his condition improving ever so slightly each day, even though he's still hanging on to life by a thread. He remains in extremely critical condition, and the doctors are putting on a full court press to save him, which they now seem to think is actually possible.

Alex has brought her laptop from home so I can read the scores of e-mails that are arriving daily from friends and well-wishers who are praying for Bernie. Each and every e-mail makes me cry with gratitude, as I can truly feel the prayers and love of others carrying us along. I'm also able to write another "Bernie Update" now that I have access to a computer for the first time since leaving home. I send the following note to the hundreds of people who are now on the e-mail list, with more writing daily asking to be included in the updates.

Bernie Update: December 31, 2008, 3:41 p.m.

Dear Friends,

First of all let me say thank you for all of the love, support and prayers during the last week. We have felt the grace of God very profoundly during this trial, and I am sure it is because of the thousands of prayers that are being offered on our behalf. We are counting on your continued prayers and we are still asking God for Bernie's complete recovery.

As of last night, Bernie is still in very critical but stable condition. The doctors here are trying everything to get his heart to come out of shock, including putting him on a ventilator, heart pump and dialysis. That means that he is completely dependent on life support right now, but the doctors assure me his condition is still reversible.

We have had several scary events where we thought we were losing him, but they immediately addressed each one with a new intervention and he improved. It has been an ongoing series of peaks and valleys. True to his personality, Bernie is continuing to fight against the odds, and I have never known Bernie to give up a fight easily. That will serve him well in this battle for his life. I know that God's grace and healing power are carrying him and us right now, and it has been remarkable to see him rebound after he has been anointed. That has happened several times now. We are so grateful for the presence of our wonderful priests, and also for the many demonstrations of love from our family and friends.

Kara, Alex and Kerry are keeping watch with me at Bernie's side, and we are determined to stay next to him until he is healed. I am asking for a miracle through the intercession of John Paul II and ask you to pray for his intercession on Bernie's behalf.

Much love and many thanks.

Judy

Sometime in the evening, we retire to the hotel again. My dear friend Cecil meets us there with a wonderful bag of dinner and snacks from Whole Foods, plus a bottle of chilled champagne in case we get the urge to toast the New Year. It seems like a good idea to me to make a toast that 2009 will somehow be better for us than 2008 was, even though it seems highly unlikely at the moment.

"Here's hoping that Dad gets better and that this New Year can somehow be salvaged," I say lifting my glass in the air to the girls. "On second thought, here's to the crappiest New Year we've ever had," I say glumly but more honestly. "And I hate to even imagine what the rest of the year is going to bring."

January 2, 2009

The New Year brings us a new cardiologist and we learn that Dr. Meiser switches with his partner, Dr. Vittorio Villandia, every two weeks for hospital duty while the other partner takes over the office. The girls and I are delighted with the change, as this new doctor is Latin and he reminds us all of Bernie.

"We have to be optimistic, but we don't want to be stupid!" Dr. Villandia tells us over and over again in his thick Honduran accent, while assuring us confidently that Bernie can still recover from this trauma. He is a breath of fresh air in this depressing place and the girls immediately develop a crush on him. All of us wait eagerly for the waft of his wonderful cologne announcing that he's arrived in the hall, and as he stands over Bernie's bed speaking to him the native Spanish they share, I feel the first shred of hope that Bernie may actually wake up.

"We want to wake him up so he can get strong enough to receive a heart transplant," Villandia says enthusiastically, as he flips his long gray shag behind his neck with dramatic effect. "Bernardo...Bernardo," he says loudly to Bernie in the name his mother still calls him "¿Puedes oírme?" which means "Can you hear me?" in Spanish. "Apriete la mano si me oye," he continues as he grabs Bernie's hand, asking Bernie for a squeeze if he can hear him. Though Bernie doesn't move a muscle, I sense intuitively that he will eventually respond to this stranger who seems so familiar to me, and I'm more than a little grateful that Bernie is in his care.

Meanwhile, the pace has slowed down somewhat in Bernie's room, and one person at a time is allowed to stay there with me now. Kerry, Kara and Alex take turns sitting with Bernie and me, and we are developing a daily routine of visitation and prayer with him. We start the day with the Rosary, and then say the morning prayers from the "Magnificat," a pocket-sized monthly magazine that contains an abbreviated form of the Divine Office—the psalms and Scripture readings prayed around the entire world in the Catholic Church each day. We continue with the Mass readings at noon and Vespers in the evening, just as they are spaced by the Church throughout the day to impregnate the day

80

with prayer. In between the readings, we bless Bernie and his room with holy water, and then we pray novenas to a variety of special saints who we're calling upon for help. One particular novena that we've begun to pray daily is the Novena to the Infant Jesus of Prague, which has been brought to the hospital by Bernie's former executive assistant Kathy.

"Someone gave this to me years ago and told me never to use it unless it's an emergency," Bernie had told me of the Infant Jesus of Prague Novena. Though Bernie has kept the prayer card with the novena on it in his desk drawer since I've known him, he brought it out only once ten years ago when he prayed it at the bedside of a dying childhood friend who had lost his faith in God.

"This is definitely an emergency," I say with relief to Kathy as she delivers the prayer card to the hospital. "We can use all of the help we can get," I tell her, and we add the novena to the long litany of prayers we are offering daily for Bernie's healing.

Bernie continues to improve and Dr. Villandia begins to back him off of both the "pressers" that are keeping his blood pressure up and the oxygen on his ventilator, which is assisting him in breathing. He's also talking about trying to wean him off of both forms of life support so we can begin to move in the direction of a heart transplant.

"We have to be optimistic, but we don't want to be stupid!" Villandia reminds me when I get too far ahead of myself in planning for Bernie to get well. Though the charismatic doctor has given us hope, he is well aware that the fight for Bernie's life is still tenuous and he gently reminds me every day that things could still turn on a dime. In spite of those admonishments, I'm becoming convinced that Bernie is going to wake up and get well, and the mood is beginning to lighten around here. Thanks to Kara, who has somehow inherited her father's sense of humor, we've even managed to laugh a few times lately.

We've giggled particularly hard over Kara's dramatic impressions of Dr. Villandia, whom she nails with exact precision in a thick Spanish accent as she imitates his nervous habit of zipping his sweater up and down while he speaks: "Come on girls, we have to be optimistic, but we don't want to be stupid!!!" she says, flipping her hair back as I laugh. I remind her that someone asked Bernie not long ago how we have survived so many difficult ordeals and he said without flinching: "laughter." And as we have experienced too many times lately, there's a fine line between laughing and crying.

Though we're advised to keep Benjamin away from the hospital to spare him the trauma of seeing his father so sick, he continues to play and ride his dirt bike in the street with his friends, thanks to Jo Jo and the neighbors who are looking after him. Meanwhile, Gaby comes to visit me at the hospital with the baby, and though Baby James is not allowed to enter Bernie's room, I proudly show off our new grandson to the CICU nurses who pass through the waiting room while Gaby spends time with Bernie. Bragging about my new grandbaby, like any other grandmother, feels like the first piece of normalcy in these long eleven days, and I relish kissing James all over his beautiful little face, wishing Bernie could wake up and see his grandson. Christian comes and goes less frequently now and I am deeply concerned about his mental health. I fear that he has relapsed completely at this point, and all I can do is surrender him to God over and over again, knowing that it isn't time to address that crisis right now.

In the meantime, I pen another update and my tone is growing more hopeful.

Bernie Update: Friday, January 2, 2009, 1:33 p.m.

Dear Friends:

As of today, January 2, Bernie continues to make slight improvements. They have reduced his oxygen on the ventilator and his blood pressure medicine, with the goal being to back him off of his ventilator completely if possible. The doctor is hopeful that he can try that in the next few days if Bernie continues to improve. According to what Dr. Villandia said yesterday morning, they are trying to get him stable enough to move toward a heart transplant. That would require getting him awake, stronger and able to undergo surgery for a mechanical heart pump. We

82

are not there yet. I am still asking the Lord for a complete healing of his heart, which would require a miracle but is not outside the spectrum of possibilities. This is not an exact science and the doctors admit that sometimes there are positive outcomes that they can't explain. God is so much bigger than all of this.

Meanwhile, Kerry, Kara, Alex and I keep vigil. We watch and pray with Bernie, and we have had many beautiful graced filled moments. The girls are singing to him in harmony throughout the day, which is absolutely beautiful and blesses everyone who hears. I am much consoled by the faith of these beautiful young women, and we continue to be hopeful that Bernie will come home with us.

Many biblical stories have come alive for me these last few days, especially that of the Israelites wandering in the desert. We are wandering through an unfamiliar place doing something we never expected, but God is providing for all we need. Our eyes are on Him and we huddle together when the night comes and the darkness tries to encroach upon us.

I could never express my gratitude for the prayers, love and support we have received, especially from my parents, sisters and neighbors who have physically and emotionally assisted us through this long eleven days. Benjamin is still playing in the street throughout the day with his little posse of friends thanks to our neighbors Jill and Michelle, and Gaby is doing a wonderful job caring for our new blessing Baby James. God's timing is so amazing.

Keep praying.

Much love,

Judy

January 6, 2009

Feast of the Epiphany

The morning brings the bad news that Bernie's fever is back and Dr. Villandia believes he has developed sepsis, a blood infection that will kill him if not arrested. His fever spiked to 104 degrees during the night and he is still unresponsive, plus he has developed a large, open bedsore on his lower back from lying in the same position for over two weeks. Worse, he's had an allergic reaction to a blood thinner called Heparin, and the tops of his hands and feet have exploded with three-inch round open wounds.

I am struck absolutely speechless when I walk into his room to find my husband lying there with what looks like the sacred wounds of Our Lord on his hands and feet. The image of the suffering Jesus is clearly stamped into Bernie's broken body, seemingly confirmed by a constant stream of bloody tears rolling down his face. Though I'm pierced to the heart by his likeness to Christ crucified, I cannot get any words out of my mouth. Kara, who is standing next to me, looks at me with disbelief on her face and utters in a shocked whisper, "Mom, Dad has the wounds of Christ!!!"

"I know," is all I can say as I stand and observe, dumbstruck by the profundity of the image. "I bear the marks of Jesus on my body," I hear in my mind, as I remember St. Paul's words in Galatians 6:17.

"What are you doing here, Lord?" I ask, wondering if Bernie could possibly look any sicker. Whatever joviality we experienced the past few days disappears into thin air as they ice Bernie's body down and set up large electric fans to blow on him continuously in an attempt to get his temperature down. Hedy comes by to visit and her strong emotional reaction tells me that she, too, is stunned by how Bernie looks. Their older brother Henry also arrives, having been prevented from coming until now due to his own hip replacement surgery two weeks ago, and all he can say is "My God, this is terrible." Though it would be hard to see anyone in this condition, it's particularly disarming to see Bernie like this, given the fact that he was such a strong, robust man only weeks ago. It's obvious to me that this is indeed the "baseball bat" of which Fr. Bendsome spoke and that Bernie has literally been knocked completely helpless by it, laid bare and humbled by a massive and unexpected jolt to his heart and the subsequent disintegration of his body.

Dr. Villandia tries to reassure me that we have not lost this battle yet, and that he will pull every trick out of his hat to try to save Bernie, whose condition he remains firmly convinced, is still reversible. "Besides," the doctor insists, "he is a young man, with a young family. We have to try to save him." Though I'm not sure what to believe anymore, I'm determined to continue to pray. I call my friend Fr. Beau to come and anoint Bernie again, then arrange for a visit from the relic of Blessed Francis Xavier Seelos, whose traveling remains have effected many miraculous cures in the sick.

The Infant Jesus of Prague Novena continues in earnest now, and our friend Kathy comes to the hospital to pray it with Bernie every thirty minutes for nine straight hours. His room has become a tabernacle of prayer, and we're blessed with visits throughout the day from family and friends who wish to intercede for him. Even the doctors and nurses join in the fray and surprise us with their constant assurances that they and their families are praying for Bernie too. "Pray and don't worry," I remind myself constantly of Padre Pio's well-known saying. Though it's easier said than done not to worry, the prayer part we can do.

The day is long and draining, but Bernie somehow makes it through. Around 11:00 p.m., I retire to Jo Jo's house, which is ten minutes away and where I moved a few days ago after the nurses insisted that I need a long-term plan because we're going to be here "for a long, long time." I end the day with a "Bernie Update" then fall into bed completely spent. Though I've been forced to surrender control over "being with Bernie if he dies," I call the hospital throughout the night to make sure he hasn't taken a downhill turn that will bring me back to his side.

Bernie Update: Tuesday, January 6, 11:00 p.m.

Dear Friends:

Bernie has continued to make baby steps forward all week, and sadly he had a setback last night. He developed a fever and the doctor thinks he may be septic. His lines will be changed tomorrow to try to locate the source of infection. They have started him on more antibiotics and are hopeful he can overcome this latest obstacle. Bernie was a Marine and his mantra is always "one hill at a time." That has truly become my mantra as well. Every hill we overcome is another step toward healing.

Yesterday they removed all of his sedation and we tried all day to wake him up. He was slightly responsive and tried to turn his head toward me when I spoke. He is much weaker and non-responsive today, probably due to the infection. Tomorrow the Dr. thinks the sedation should be out of his system and hopefully the fever will have abated. If he does not wake up, neurological tests will be ordered. They have been operating under the assumption that he is neurologically sound and he is too critical to move for a CAT scan. Please pray that his infection clears up and that his kidneys start to work, as they are totally shut down at the moment. Also pray that he becomes alert and responsive.

Fr. Beau came and anointed Bernie again today. My friend Maria's mother also came with the relic of Blessed Seelos and prayed over him so beautifully for healing. Bernie's friend Kathy came and prayed the novena to the Infant Jesus of Prague every half hour with him throughout the day. He is covered in prayer and love and I am sure he knows that we are all present and interceding for him.

Hopefully tomorrow will bring good news. Meanwhile, we wait on the Lord as he helps us walk minute by minute through this trial. Your many e-mails and phone calls have been a source of hope and consolation, as are the constant stream of meals that arrive at our home.

Much love,
Judy

January 8, 2009

Feast of our Lady of Prompt Succor

Today is the feast of Our Lady of Prompt Succor, a day beloved by many New Orleanians who honor Our Lady by attending a solemn Mass at her Shrine at Ursuline Academy, the oldest continuously-operating school for women in the United States. Thankfully, Bernie's fever has broken and the doctors appear to have gotten his infection under control. He is more alert today than he's been since they put him on the ventilator two weeks ago and, amazingly, he opens his eyes and appears to make eye contact with me then responds to my questions by blinking! And miracle of miracles, he's no longer "the sickest patient in Louisiana!" That is a great leap forward considering that his odds of victory over death were much less than the three to one that Andrew Jackson and his soldiers faced this very day almost two hundred years ago when they defeated the British at the Battle of New Orleans because Our Lady of Prompt Succor interceded to bring them to victory.

"Our Lady of Prompt Succor, hasten to help us!" we continue to pray as we wait for Bernie to become completely alert and responsive, which the doctors tell us could take another week. When that happens, the plan is to take him off the ventilator and insert a temporary tracheostomy so he can begin to speak. Since we have had virtually no communication since December 26 other than the few blinks of his eyes today, the thought of talking to Bernie again is beginning to feel like dream that may come true, and I'm anxiously awaiting the opportunity to ask him if he's seen Jesus, which I'm completely convinced he has.

Feeling encouraged and hopeful, I drive home for the first time in two weeks to spend the night and check on all of the kids. I'm half-reminded as I see baby gear upon entering the house that we now have an infant living here, and I'm filled with joy at the thought of getting to know this new little person who has entered our lives. It warms my heart to see what a wonderful job Gaby is doing caring for James, and to witness what attentive and competent parents she and Grayson are is a welcome relief. Any concerns I had about the how the two of them would handle so much responsibility have completely abated. I'm now persuaded that if they can maintain their composure in this pressure-packed situation, they'll do just fine with the rest of the challenges life may present.

Benjamin has returned to school and Grayson is preparing to go back to college for the spring semester. Alex and Kara have put their lives on hold so they can alternate between helping Jo Jo at home and sitting with me at the hospital, as the days are long and tedious for all of us and it helps to have a companion present to ward off the isolation. Christian is spending most of his time with friends in Covington, and I pray constantly that he will make it alive through this calamity. Although I teeter back and forth between fear and peace intermittently, I'm beginning to have more peace than fear as I practice surrendering to God each and every minute of the day. I have an incredible sense that God is taking care of us and my trust in Him is growing daily.

"Maybe this is what victory looks like," I think to myself as I remember the prophecy spoken over me at Fr. Jerry's healing retreat in November, when I was seen in a vision as a victor and not a victim for the first time in my life. Considering that I do not feel victimized by this latest catastrophe in our lives and that I feel an inexplicable peace and confidence in God that far surpasses my understanding, I am convinced that I must have experienced a miracle at that wonderful healing retreat. I can honestly say that I feel oddly hopeful—even strangely joyful—during many moments right now, and I'm experiencing the palpable presence of God in a way I've never known before. When I reflect on the grip that fear and mistrust have had on me for years, the shift in me is incomprehensible outside of the grace of God. I tear out a page from the daily "Magnificat" readings and tape it on the refrigerator in the kitchen. It says:

"God indeed is my savior; I am confident and unafraid. My strength and my courage is the LORD, and he has been my savior." (Isaiah 12:2-3)

Those words at long last ring true to me, and it is such a relief to believe them.

January 16, 2009

Dr. Meiser has returned to the hospital for rounds and has resumed his role as the lead physician on Bernie's case. He manages to back Bernie off of his sedation completely and, incredibly, Bernie wakes up and is able to answer questions by nodding his head. He communicates that he remembers having a heart attack and says he's not in pain. As the day progresses, he lifts his head off the pillow and even squeezes my hand. It seems that he is making progress by the hour, and when Dr. Meiser removes the balloon pump from his heart in the afternoon, his blood pressure and heart rate remain strong and steady for several hours.

By late afternoon, the pulmonologist, who's in charge of Bernie's lungs, lets Bernie breathe for two hours off the ventilator, which is the first step in weaning him off of it completely. He made it through the entire two hours without an incident despite working hard to catch his breath, and was alert and responsive to questions afterwards. He even managed to move his hands and his feet several times today, not noticing the unhealed open wounds still present on the tops of both. This is much more progress than we dreamed possible when we arrived here on December 28 and got the horrifying news that Bernie was in total organ failure and "probably wouldn't make it through the night."

The staff in the CICU considers Bernie's headway nothing short of miraculous and has even begun calling him "Miracle Man." Every doctor, nurse and medical technician who enters his room tells us that his remarkable recovery is the talk of the hospital, and each conveys their amazement that Bernie is awake and communicative since "he was basically dead when he arrived here," as one nurse bluntly put it. A physician named Dr. Aballah assures me it's a miracle that Bernie is alive and shares that he is confident that God will bring him the rest of the way through prayer. A female nurse comes into the room and belts out "Amazing Grace" in a voice so anointed and sweet that it transports me to heaven temporarily as I close my eyes and enter into the worship of God with a sister in Christ whom I met only minutes ago.

I'm deeply appreciative, yet somewhat surprised, to find such open displays of faith among the medical community here, and their service to us at this vulnerable moment in our lives drives home to me the reality that health care is truly a sacred ministry. Though I've told my students many times about the monks who cared for the sick in the monasteries of Europe, which were called "hospitalliers" and eventually gave rise to hospitals in the Western world, the faith of the doctors and nurses that surround us in this place testifies to me that medicine is indeed a God-given vocation. I'm wondering if overt demonstrations of faith are common in other hospitals around the country or if this is unique in largely Catholic New Orleans.

Notwithstanding the new challenges that present themselves constantly, such as having to shock Bernie's heart twice this morning to help it recover from arrhythmia, there is a significant improvement in his overall condition, and I now believe that he is going to get well and come home with us. As I share my conviction with those around me that Bernie is going to "walk out of here with us," Dr. Meiser relays his concern to me that I am "too optimistic" about my husband's recovery. And, while I assure the doctor that I'm using a figure of speech because I understand that Bernie will need a wheelchair when he leaves the hospital, he cautions me not to get my hopes too high, as his improving state of health can reverse itself at any minute.

It's hard for me to navigate the tightrope between real hope that Bernie is getting better and clear-headed awareness that he could still die on any given day. He is improving, but he is not out of the woods. He's much better than when we arrived, but he still is in very critical, albeit stable, condition. I am leaning on the side of positive expectation for his complete recovery while Dr. Meiser tries to pull me back to the center where I stay clear on the fact that Bernie has a long, long road to go to recovery, and that road includes a heart transplant, which he's still too sick to receive. The pull between hope and caution reminds me that in medicine, just like in theology, right belief lies in the mean between the two extremes, and that real tension exists in the middle of the two positions which must simply be embraced.

Though I feel the tension between "optimism" and "stupidity," the fact that I feel very positive, and even joyful, a majority of the time these days is a marvel to me, especially since I've leaned to the side of gripping fear, mistrust and anxiety for most of my life and rarely toward hopeful optimism. My major conversion experience when I was twenty-three-years-old did, thanks be to God, propel me from agnosticism to a personal relationship with Christ. But that conversion did not remedy a deep-seated, unspoken belief that God can't really be trusted no matter how much faith I have, nor the a fundamental sense of being unsafe that has assailed my mind and heart throughout my life. Bernie has rightly and regularly accused me for years of being "so damn negative," and the tragic events of the past few years have poured fuel on the firewall within me that has kept God out of the deepest recesses of my heart.

But now something has changed. The trust and hope I feel in the midst of the most difficult personal challenge I have ever faced in my life is evidence of an internal shift that is profound and real, and no one is more surprised about it than me. I want to shake Dr. Meiser by his shoulders and yell "Too optimistic??? You just don't know me!!! Don't you know that this hope I'm feeling is a miracle?!" Knowing he will never understand, I tuck my hope back into my heart and enjoy it on my own.

Hedy's daughters Annie and Leah arrive from Wyoming and Washington D.C. They bring my ninety-year-old, now senile mother-in-law Letty to the hospital to see her son and to pray.

"Bernardito...Papito lindo, lo que te pasó?" she says with confusion on her face, trying to comprehend what has happened to her son. "What happened to him?" she asks over and over again in broken English as we take turns telling her repeatedly that Bernardo suffered a heart attack.

"Bernardo's going to be okay, Senora," I tell her with confidence, believing it to be true. My nieces remark that they are amazed at the peace they experience while visiting their uncle, and we take turns blessing him with holy water before we join our voices and hearts together in prayer.

"I'm learning that it truly is a gift to visit the sick and usher them to holiness through prayer," Annie shares with me after we leave Bernie's room. The mystery is that we are all being ushered more deeply into God's presence as we pray and believe for Bernie's healing, as it seems that the more we pray for him, the more peace and inner healing we receive, too.

When I get to Jo Jo's house, which is ten minutes from the hospital, I write another update to family and friends, trying to give them a sense of the atmosphere of faith and hope in Bernie's room.

Bernie Update: January 16, 2009, 11:30 p.m.

Hi Friends:

Bernie breathed off the ventilator for two hours today and he is doing well and resting peacefully. The last few days presented several new challenges, including having to shock his heart twice to help it recover a normal rhythm. My nieces (Annie and Leah) arrived from DC and Jackson Hole last night and we, along with Bernie's mother Letty, prayed with Bernie until 11:00 p.m. tonight. Apparently the prayers are working, as the doctors say there is a significant improvement in his lung x-ray and breathing function. Praise God! They are hoping to place a temporary tracheostomy in immediately and are foregoing plans to put in a feeding tube in the hopes he can start eating food next week

Meanwhile, the doctor has shared his concern that I am "too optimistic" about Bernie's recovery. Most days, I have been completely convinced he is going get well and "walk out of here with us" (I told the doctor this is a figure of speech...I understand he will probably need a wheelchair when he leaves). The fact that I have felt very positive the majority of the time is evidence of the grace of God and the thousands of prayers that are being prayed for us. That and my mother's firmly convinced voice that tells me every day "He is going to get well. Believe it!"

The doctors and nurses at Ochsner have been wonderful. I can't say enough about their hard work and kindness. The neurologist (female) came in and cried yesterday as I was telling her about Benjamin and showing her the pictures of the children posted all over the walls. She was visibly moved. About ten minutes later another nurse came in and sang "Amazing Grace" for me in the most anointed voice. Every nurse in the hall asks about Bernie's progress, and many hug me as I go by and say they are praying, their parents are praying, their children are praying! I know we are not alone...so many friends near and far are carrying us with their love and prayers.

Bernie has come so far (truly a miracle!) and he still has a long way to go. We are counting on your continued prayers.

Blessings and love,

Judy

January 23, 2009

Today marks Bernie's one month anniversary in the hospital and there is no immediate end in sight. He has lost sixty pounds and I've lost ten, and this is one hell of a way to go on a diet. In reality, I cried quite of few tears when they weighed Bernie and I saw how much weight he's lost in a month. It's terribly unnerving to see my husband becoming a shadow of his former self, and it's another reminder of just how sick he still is. Today also brings the disheartening news that Bernie's lungs are beginning to look cloudy again, which is especially disappointing considering he's been breathing mostly on his own since they weaned him off the ventilator during the day and put a tracheostomy tube in for him to breathe through a couple of days ago. I'm learning that having a serious infirmity is somewhat of a roller-coaster ride and, believe me, the famous Zephyr at Pontchartrain Beach Amusement Park was nothing compared to this.

"Two steps forward, one step backward," my sister Renee reminds me when she sees the discouragement on my face. Every nurse knows that's the way it is when one is gravely ill.

"You need to get him out of this hospital as soon as possible, Judy," my sister advises me, knowing from experience that the longer a person stays in the hospital, the higher the risk that they'll die of a hospital related complication such as an infection or pneumonia. With that in mind, I ask the physical therapist to teach me the exercises to help strengthen Bernie's body, knowing that it will take a monumental effort to rebuild his strength and muscle tone, as his muscles are completely atrophied and he can still barely lift any part of his body off the bed.

The silver lining in the clouds is that Bernie *was* successfully weaned off the ventilator and is breathing on his own except at night, which is no small feat considering that he was in total lung failure when we arrived here and spent almost a month with a breathing tube down his throat. The doctors are hoping that his vocal cords are not damaged from being intubated for so long, and they're moving toward getting him to speak in the next week or so, provided that his lungs clear up and that they're strong enough for him to exert his voice.

Though Bernie can't talk audibly yet, he is smiling frequently now and has begun to mouth words to me. I'm having a crash course in lip reading, which is very frustrating at times for both of us, but I'm getting better at it every day. Talk about appreciating the small victories in life—I never knew I would be so excited to figure out a word! I'm trying to decode and answer all of his questions, which include wanting to know what happened to him, how long he'll be in the hospital, how the kids are and when he'll see the baby. He's also started asking for kisses and mouthed to me today that we need to get going with physical therapy. Though physical therapy has already begun, he's anxious to get moving, even though he is still sedated and asleep the majority of the time.

Many people are writing now to ask how *I'm* doing and, by the grace of God, I can honestly say I feel peaceful and quite hopeful most of the time—which I'm always aware is *my* miracle. But I must confess that there are very difficult moments too, where the reality of this situation hits me hard and I fall apart like a cheap suit, and usually in front of others. I had one of those occasions tonight when I came home to visit for the second time, and had a meltdown in the kitchen because the floor needed to be mopped and there was tomato sauce all over the kitchen cabinets. As I mopped the floor, crying, "I don't want to eat that stupid hospital food any more!!!" nine-year old Benjamin walked into the kitchen and announced, "Okay, Mom, you're having one of those overly dramatic moments!" Though poor Kara and Gaby thought I had morphed into "Mommy Dearest," Benjamin unwittingly offered necessary comic relief and we all cracked up.

The truth is that "life is hawd" right now, to coin my mother's famous saying in a mock New Orleans Ninth Ward accent. We are all carrying a heavy cross at the moment, and we're each doing our best to hold up under it. I still need a good, hard cry on a regular basis, and though I'm no longer assailed by crippling fear, I do struggle with deep sadness about this whole situation as I try mightily to "accept the things I cannot change."

I keep hearing the voice of our son Christian as it echoes in my ears, remembering when we moved into our current home in Beau Chene when he was only four. He seemed totally disoriented by the change, and for the first two weeks, he walked around with a pitiful look on his face saying over and over again, "I want to go home!!!" That's how I honestly feel, and if I could close my eyes, click my heels and zap us all back home, I would do it in an instant. I yearn to go home and bring my husband with me, but I can't, so I go back to the hospital for another day of watching, waiting and praying. The days are long and fatiguing, but the discovery of the chapel on the first floor of the hospital has provided a refuge for me to gather my thoughts in silence. The other major consolation I have is that either a priest or a Eucharistic minister brings me the Eucharist daily, and I look forward to this superabundant food—my daily bread—to sustain me for another day.

The hospital chaplain comes in often, and he administers the Sacrament of the Sick to Bernie every time he has a setback, which is not infrequent considering the ongoing issues with his heart, lungs, kidneys, open wounds and infections. "Two steps forward, and one step backward," Renee reminds me again. When I think about it...that *is* still progress, isn't it?

January 29, 2009

The bill collectors have started to pounce, and they are calling nonstop as I try to negotiate payments from the hospital room while Bernie sleeps. One small blessing in disguise has been the nation's home mortgage crisis and related stock market crash, which has given me, along with the thousands of other financially strapped people in our country, the unexpected opportunity to renegotiate our mortgage payments. If I thought our finances had tanked before this plight hit, I can only imagine that we will be destitute before it's over with. Though we have an abundance of every kind of insurance imaginable, we've never taken the time or trouble to get disability insurance, as we never expected anything to happen to Bernie's health. It's glaringly obvious to me now that that's the one kind of insurance we really should have had, as Bernie's sudden cessation of all work is nothing short of financially catastrophic for us. Sadly, that realization is too little, too late, and the bills continue to mount.

Thank God for the generosity of our family members, who have begun showing up unasked at the hospital with cash and checks. Bernie's brother Henry puts a wad of cash in my palm as I kiss him goodbye after a visit, and Hedy comes with a large contribution to carry us through. My mother Phyllis meets me in the waiting room with a check tucked inside a gift for me, assuring me there's more where that came from if I need it.

"I had planned to wait until you finished your PhD to give you this," she says as she hands me the diamond cross my father gave her on their wedding night, which she knows is the one piece of her jewelry I've always wanted. "But I think you've earned it now because you've been such an example of Jesus to everyone around you." I cry sincere tears of appreciation for those words, which mean everything to me coming from my mother. Although we've had some rough spots in our relationship, she has become my hero in recent years, as I've watched her deal so courageously with the deaths of her two sons: the murder-suicide of my brother Stephen and his wife Brenda, and the suicide of Scott, who became a cocaine addict when he was barely a teen and killed himself in despair over his addiction when he was only thirty-five.

My mother, who has always loved children and "wanted a dozen," ended up with seven boys and three girls in eleven years. Our home was always full of children, and she considered it her duty to care for the neglected kids of others. Over the years, she would "adopt" a number of boys whose mothers were mentally ill, with one even living in our renovated basement with my brothers for a year during high school. The remarkable thing was that my mother never even mentioned it or acted like it was unusual in any way to care for the children of others. She would bring her "adopted sons" along most everywhere we went, including summer vacations and shopping for shoes, where they got a new pair, too, without a word of complaint from her.

There was rarely a night that we didn't have extra people at our dinner table growing up, even though it took great time and effort to prepare a meal for our family of twelve, which included seven hungry, growing boys. If the food were running short, my mother would say to us in code: "FHB." We knew that meant "family hold back," so our guests would have enough to eat. But there was usually plenty of food to go around, which she cooked in massive cast iron pots in our hot, un-air conditioned kitchen. You could smell the delectable aroma of Southern specialties like fried pork chops and breaded veal—which was known in New Orleans as "pane' meat"—filling the streets through the open screen windows of our home. The clanging of the six o'clock church bells from St. James the Major Church three blocks away meant that dinner was served. And you'd better be on time or else.

Despite the fact that my mother stopped claiming any religious belief over forty years ago, I say that she's a Christian who walks the walk without talking the talk, and I wish I were more like her. Her response to my brothers' deaths is a perfect example of her bravery in the face of great suffering, and though I rib her about giving me "big shoes to stand in," I'm all too aware it's true. Instead of letting the brutal blow of her two sons' suicides destroy her, she's used her grief to help others who are less fortunate to attain better lives. After Scott's death, she founded the Children's Advocacy Center to help teachers recognize and report the signs of sexual abuse in children. Following the deaths of Stephen and Brenda, she went on to co-found the Mahalia Jackson Center for Early Childhood Development, which is designed to pull children and their families out of the cycle of poverty.

Though people have been amazed over the years at her drive and passion to help children, she shared her secret motive with Bernie after his son Marshall's death, encouraging him to use his grief as an impetus for good instead of letting it defeat him. She would write the following words to Bernie, encouraging him to move forward into the light, sharing her own temptation to close the curtains and become "a woman dressed in black" before she found a way out of her personal hell by reaching out to others:

Dearest Bernie....

At first after Scott's death, I wanted to remove myself from all my activities, pull down into the lonely darkness. I resigned from all the boards I was on and stopped attending many social activities. I wanted to just sit and hold my pain.

But the abused children kept calling me, and I found an opportunity out of the darkness by working to open the Children's Advocacy Center. I did it in Scott's name and there is a picture of Scott on the wall. My associates in my Task Force seemed to understand and support me. If I could relieve some child's suffering, I could relieve some of Scott's suffering, and mine. Little by little, it worked. Every day I keep moving in the direction of the children. There are so many suffering, just as I am, with pain and disappointment. In helping them, I am helping myself. And opportunities continue to come. They dim my pain, and I am rejoicing that Scott is in some way helping them also.

This is my story, never told before. Each time I feel sorrow, I look around for someone to help or I think lovingly of someone. I am thinking lovingly of you, now. Open your eyes. There is a path for you. Carry Marshall on your shoulders as you walk out into life. Bit by bit move toward the light. Take hold and go forward. Your grief can be your banner and it will make you special.

Love,

Phyllis

My mother reminds me every day "where there's life, there's hope." She also tells me daily not to give up the fight because "Bernie's going to get better...believe it!!!" I hold that thought in my mind as I arrange for Benjamin to come visit him for the first time today and fret over how it will affect our child to see his father so disabled. Dr. Villandia, who's back on duty, suggests that he meet with the Family Life Therapist first so she can prepare him for what he is going to see in Bernie's room.

Benjamin arrives at the hospital with Bernie's granddaughters Kaylie and Emily, who buried their own father Marshall when they were nine and seven, respectively, after seeing him comatose and connected to life support. They've all been through an awful lot and the therapist gives them a chance to talk about how they feel. They're scared and sad, they tell her, and anxious about how Bernie is doing and when he's coming home. Then they color banners for Bernie's room that say "Get Well Soon" and "We Love You" as I stand in the corner with tears rolling down my face thinking how cruel life can be.

The tension is high as we all hold hands and enter the room together, but it dissipates immediately when Bernie blows the children kisses and mouths "I love you" to all of them. Though "Opa," which is the German name for grandfather that the kids call Bernie, is still barely able to move from the neck down, being in his presence is welcome relief for all and having the children come visit is "one more hill" among many that we have crossed.

"When can I come back and visit again, Mommy?" Benjamin asks as he leaves.

"Any time you want to," I tell him sincerely, wondering how many more visits it will take until Bernie can come home and how much emotional trauma our baby boy will sustain before this is over with.

February 1, 2009

This morning brings Bernie's first words since the tracheostomy tube was inserted into his neck. The speech therapist came by yesterday to measure the tube for a plastic cap that enables him to force air through his voice box and out of his mouth when the tube is covered up. The clear, round cap arrives first thing in the morning and is installed by a nurse while I'm away taking care of personal business. Bernie's first sentence is thus directed to Jo Jo, who is sitting with him while I am gone.

"Where's my wife?!" are the first three words he speaks in thirty-eight days. Of course he would begin speaking during a rare moment when I wasn't in his room! My sister immediately calls to tell me, "You'd better get back here quickly! Bernie's awake and speaking and he's asking where you are. Hurry up and get here!" she insists.

"Oh my God, I'm on my way!!" I say in an excited panic, upset that I have missed his first words, yet thrilled that he is speaking. I race back to the hospital to find Bernie speaking in a clear voice, sounding surprisingly like his old self in spite of all he's been through. Remarkably, his voice is strong and the speech therapist is delighted that he endured so many weeks with a tube down his throat with no apparent damage to his vocal cords.

"Bernardo, I can't even believe you're speaking!!!" I say in an exuberant voice as I breeze past the nurse and stand beside his bed. "Do you have any idea how long we've all been waiting for this?" I ask as joyful tears run from my eyes.

"What happened to me?" he asks with a frustrated look on his face that tells me he's been anxiously holding questions inside that I failed to understand through lip reading. "Tell me everything that happened," he continues as I pull my chair close to his bed and hold his hand so I can give him a brief synopsis of the last six weeks, leaving out the part about how close he came to dying to avoid scaring him. I recount that he had a heart attack after the stress test, and that Dr. Madden opened his blocked stents, but that his heart went into shock right after Christmas. I tell him that he was transferred to Ochsner on December 28 and that the doctors here have fought aggressively to help him get better. I guard my words so as not to frighten him while trying to convey what a miracle it is that he is awake and speaking.

"What month is this?" he questions, looking very confused, as the day, month and year have all changed since he got sick.

"It's February 1st, honey. Two thousand and nine. You had a heart attack six weeks ago, and you've been unconscious since right after Christmas," I continue gingerly, as I can see the fear and confusion on his face.

"When am I going home?" he wants to know.

"I don't know, honey," I answer honestly and sadly. "You need to get strong enough to go home. We need to continue to focus on getting you better so you can come home."

He tells me how thirsty he is and the doctor agrees to let me give him ice chips, which is quite a treat considering he hasn't eaten anything since December 26. As the day progresses, the doctor allows me to give him a spoonful of Sprite, which Bernie announces is "delicious." The medical team is talking about moving him into a special chair tomorrow that will accommodate sitting up and more physical therapy. Since he still can't move from the neck down, other than lifting his hands and head and wiggling his feet, it will take a team of physical therapists and nurses to get him out of the bed and into the chair. Dr. Villandia has also ordered a "swallow test" to see if he's ready to begin eating real food. Though they have been feeding him a liquid supplement for several weeks via a tube that runs through his nose into his stomach, the doctor has been putting off having a feeding tube surgically installed into his stomach in the hopes he can begin to eat on his own. But first it must be determined whether he can swallow food without aspirating.

"We have to move quickly to get him stronger, because the longer he lays here not moving, the harder it's going to be to get him well," Dr. Villandia advises me in his thick Honduran accent. "We need to sit him up and get him to eat food. That will make him stronger," the doctor explains. "Once he gets strong enough, we can move him to a rehab hospital where they can work with him for several hours a day to get him out of bed and walking again," he continues. "But the first step is sitting him up and making him eat," he conveys to me as he nervously zips and unzips the neck of the thick black cardigan he is wearing, which makes me think of Kara's perfect imitation of him each time he raises his hand to the zipper.

"Bernardo," the doctor continues in the language that he and Bernie share, asking if he's hungry and if he wants something to eat. "¿Tienes hambre? ¿Quieres comer algo?"

"No, but I'll try," Bernie responds. Even though he's not the least bit hungry, he promises to try his best to eat something if the doctor thinks that will get him well. Getting him better has become the focal point of all our hopes, all our dreams, all our prayers.

The day continues with Bernie talking through the tracheostomy tube at length, obviously relieved that he can finally communicate all of the things he's been thinking as he lay flat on his back unable to speak. A glimmer of the man I once knew emerges as he begins to give me directions about what he wants. I'm thrilled that's he's starting to push, as it's the first real signal thus far that Bernie Klein is coming back!

"Get a pencil and paper to write this down," he tells me seriously as though we're sitting in his office again. "I want you to put a schedule on the wall so I know when you're coming and going every day," he says as I try to hide the smile on my face. "And you need to be more aggressive with the doctors. You're going to have to take charge of this situation if I'm going to get out of here."

"Right, honey," I say, wanting to giggle to myself, thinking that there's no way he could possibly have a clue about how aggressively we've fought this battle to save his life and how many life and death decisions "the most indecisive person in the world" has made over the past thirty-eight days on his behalf.

Bernie has a million questions, and I try to answer them all. One of the things he's most concerned about is how the baby is and how Gaby is adjusting to being a mother.

"The baby is gorgeous and healthy, honey," I tell him proudly. "And Gaby is an incredible mother. She's doing such a great job of taking care of him."

"I knew she'd be a good mother," he responds. "I knew she had it in her...and what about Grayson? Does he love the baby? Is he a good father?" he asks with concern.

"Yes, honey. He's a great father and they're taking care of the baby together," I respond.

"Good. That makes me happy," he says with relief. "I'm tired and I'm starting to feel a lot of pain," he says, becoming distracted by the chronic pain from the bedsore on his back. "Can you call the nurse and ask her to give me some pain medication?"

"Sure, honey," I answer. "But can you please tell me something that I've been waiting all of this time to ask you?"

"What is it?" he asks.

"Did you meet Jesus?" I ask quietly and expectantly.

"Yes, I did," he nods with his eyes closed.

"Well...did he speak to you?" I continue, trying to keep my intense curiosity at an appropriate level.

"He didn't speak in a language we use on this earth," is all he offers. "I can't describe it to you. I don't even know if I can articulate it," he says as he dozes off. And with that, I'm left with wonder and anticipation about what happened, hoping my husband will become clear enough to tell me the details of his encounter with Jesus in the near future.

When Bernie wakes up in the afternoon, his spirits are very low, as he's begun to process what's happened to him and is becoming more cognizant of how debilitated he is. Though I've tried to answer his questions honestly, I'm sensitive to the fact that too much information will overwhelm him right now, especially the details about how long and hard he has yet to fight in order to get out of this place. As of today, he's still dependent on life support, which includes IV drips that keep his heart rate and blood pressure at life-sustaining levels, full-time dialysis for his failed kidneys, and help breathing from the ventilator during the night, which the nurse attaches to his tracheostomy tube to assist his still-tenuous lungs. Furthermore, the doctors can't explain why he can barely move from the neck down. Despite their assurances that he would begin moving when they removed the paralyzing agent from his body, his ongoing paralysis is an unanswered neurological mystery that has caused him to become a case study among the medical students in this teaching hospital. All of that, along with his black, gangrenous fingers that ceased to have circulation in them when the "pressers" were introduced into his body to keep his heart beating, brings teams of medical students into this room all day long to observe his case.

Additionally, Bernie has been asking the doctors and nurses specific questions about his condition and his chances for recovery throughout the day, and though they've all been taking turns giving him repeated pep talks about how far he's come thus far, the discouragement is showing on his face as he gets more information about his case. I follow the lead of the medical staff by trying to answer his questions truthfully while refraining from giving him information that might alarm him, such as the fact that it's beginning to look like he will need dialysis for the rest of his life if he survives, given the extended amount of time that he's been in total kidney failure at this point.

As the day wears on, the kids and I decide that a surprise visit from the baby might bring a much-needed emotional boost, so we ask permission from the medical staff to allow Gaby to bring James into the CICU. Dr. Villandia agrees that it will help for Bernie to see his grandson, who's now six weeks old, and clearance is obtained for the baby to enter his grandfather's room for a quick visit late this afternoon.

I can hardly contain myself as Gaby crosses the threshold and announces, "Dad, this is your grandson James Gabriel," in an emotionally charged voice. Gaby and I both fight back tears as she lays James on Bernie's chest so he can get a get a good look at the baby. I know that she and I are both remembering simultaneously that her dad assured her in May that she would not do this alone because he would be there to support her every step of the way. Who knew that he wouldn't lay eyes on the child until he was a month and a half old, and that he would be too weak and sick to even hold James in his arms.

"Awww...he looks just like me," Bernie says of the dark-haired baby, even though it's plain as day that James is the spitting image of Grayson. "Is Grayson a good father, baby?" he asks Gaby with concern in his eyes.

"Yes, Dad, he's a very good father," she answers honestly.

"Good," he responds, looking exhausted and frail. "Are you nursing him?" he continues.

"Yes I am, and he's doing really well with it," she adds.

"That's great, baby. He's beautiful. I'm so proud of you. Thank you for bringing him to see me," Bernie says.

"You're welcome, Dad," she says as I tell her to get closer to Bernie so I can take a picture of the three of them together. "He'll be waiting for you when you come home," she promises with tears rolling down her cheeks as she bends down, kisses Bernie on the face and tells him that she loves him. She then puts James back into the papoose on her chest and covers his head with a blanket to protect him from germs so she can walk back down the long corridor of the CICU and leave.

After Gaby's departure, there's a definite elevation in Bernie's mood. He was thrilled to see the baby and I'm so relieved for Gaby that her dad has finally seen her child. One more hill. His spirits are also lifted by a phone conversation with Kara, who's singing at a conference in Chicago with Immaculee Ilibagiza, author of the runaway bestseller "Left to Tell." Immaculee has asked her to write some songs about the genocide in Rwanda and the apparitions of Our Lady of Kibeho, with the goal of using the songs in a movie that a famous Hollywood producer is hoping to make about the Rwandan massacre that is the subject of Immaculee's book.

Bernie, who has been Kara's manager for the past five years and produced her four CDs, wants to talk to her about her game plan and be involved in the decision making process concerning any possible career opportunities. It's excruciating to observe this man who was once bigger than life trying to put his game face on as he comes to the realization that he's completely helpless physically. Though he's doing his best to re-engage with the world around him, it takes a great deal of energy and effort on his part and he shares with me several times during the day that he's feeling very depressed. I call the psychiatrist for a consult to see if they can put him on an anti-depressant and she assures me they'll begin one immediately.

Christian comes to the hospital for a visit in the evening after learning that Bernie is speaking, and he can see that I am weary from being stretched between the pull of consolation that Bernie is alert, aware and communicative and consternation that he's now experiencing depression and anxiety as he realizes the condition he's in. It hasn't occurred to me until now that having our prayers answered for Bernie to wake up and communicate with us would force us to encounter a paradox between joy and grief, but it warms my heart as my son tries to give me comfort and courage in spite of his own fear about his father's current state.

"Mom," he offers as he puts his arm around me. "Don't worry. Dad is a soldier. He is going to keep fighting. He has never put his mind to anything that he has not accomplished and he has never given up a fight." Truer words have never been spoken, and the fight in Bernie will be a necessary and key ingredient if he is going to keep pushing forward to get well.

"You're right, Christian. Thank you for reminding me of that. I love you, son," I say as I hug him tightly, grateful that he's here with us this evening and seems to be doing okay.

When I get home to Jo Jo's at 10:30 p.m., I type out a "Bernie Update" to share the latest developments with family and friends, which include mostly positive advances in spite of the ongoing emotional challenges. It's been a very long, busy day and tomorrow is Alex's twenty-second birthday, which we still have yet to figure out how to celebrate.

Bernie Update: Sunday, February 1

Dear Friends:

Bernie has had a fantastic week overall and I pray that we're beginning to see the light at the end of the tunnel in getting out of this hospital. Instead of talking about if he is going to make it, if he is going to wake up, or if he is going to have brain damage, we are discussing what kind of rehab he will need and what facility to eventually put him in. Though it still may take several weeks for him to be able to move to a rehab center, at least we are discussing that option. We are also working on getting him to eat real food (a challenge when one has not swallowed food for thirty-eight days) and more aggressive rehab in his room. Bernie is now able to lift his hands and wrists, and the physical therapist is working on getting him to raise his arms. He is determined to get out of here as soon as possible and we all know that when his will kicks in, there is no stopping him. The remaining hurdles for him to be able to move on from here include getting his blood pressure to go up and for his dialysis to move from continuous to intermittent. Please continue to pray for his kidneys to begin to work, as they are completely shut down still.

In addition to considering rehab locations, this week has brought his first visit from Benjamin, Kaylie, Emily and the baby!!! You can imagine how thrilled he was to see his son and grandchildren. Another huge development is that he has also begun to speak, and he carried on phone conversations with various people, including my mother, who burst

106

into tears when she called and I put Bernie on the phone. He asked her "How YOU doin'?"' (a familiar joke between the two of them) in such a clear voice that she said she shook for an hour after they hung up because she was so shocked to hear him speak. He also spoke to Kara about the possibility of her recording songs for the upcoming "Left to Tell" movie. He is getting back to himself and I cannot tell you what a relief and joy it is to see him return. God willing, there will be no more setbacks and we can continue to move forward.

Since all of this began on Dec. 23, I have been reflecting on the irony of my study and teaching of Health Care Ethics and this journey through such a profound health care crisis. Part of my curriculum in the PhD program was to include a clinical experience in the hospital, and I was so grateful at the time that I didn't live in Rome and was exempt from that requirement, as I have a very weak stomach and don't do well around hospital stuff. Oh well, I guess God had other plans. I have learned much more about medical issues, medicines and patient care than I ever wanted to know. But as Msgr. Bill, a Ukrainian rite priest, psychiatrist and medical ethics expert who assists at our local parish, has said, "it will make (me) a better teacher." I sure hope so!

Peace and blessings.

Love,

Judy

February 11, 2009

Feast of our Lady of Lourdes

It's seven a.m. and I awaken in Jo Jo's guestroom crying from a terrible nightmare. I dreamed that I was in Bernie's hospital room, and that I could see my deceased brother Stephen standing at the nurses station in the hall, peering through the viewing glass at Bernie with a menacing look on his face. My sense was that he was trying to influence Bernie negatively somehow, and I could feel the spiritual oppression around me as I saw him hovering nearby and remembered him shooting himself and Brenda. "Jesus, help us," I pray, as I walk into the kitchen sobbing and shaking, unable to stave off the panic that slammed me yesterday when I got to the hospital and learned that Bernie had a major setback the night before that put him back on the ventilator for a day.

Bernie was weak and lethargic throughout the day yesterday as the ventilator breathed for him, and his blood pressure remained alarmingly low, registering at sixty over forty for an extended period of time while the nurse titrated his medicine in an attempt to bring it back up. Although he was unable to communicate with me verbally, his eyes told the tale of how disheartened he is. He was breathing on his own again by night time, but the pulmonologist advised me that it would probably take him a week to get back to where he was before fluid started gathering around his heart and lungs, causing him to "crash" and forcing him back to mechanical breathing.

As Holy Mass is the highest form of prayer on earth and we need divine intervention again, I shower and decide that I need to attend Mass at St. Francis Xavier Church across the street from Jo Jo's house before I go to the hospital. Yesterday's conversations with the doctors were rather dismal, and it is becoming apparent that Bernie has arrived at somewhat of a quagmire in his convalescence that may prove to be unresolvable. The dilemma is that Bernie needs extensive rehabilitation to get stronger and become a candidate for a heart transplant, but no rehab facility will accept him as a patient until his blood pressure elevates to a life-sustaining level without pharmaceutical assistance. Furthermore, no facility will take him unless his kidneys recover some function, as none of them are equipped to administer the continuous dialysis that he is receiving in intensive care. The problem is that his heart is just too weak to remedy the blood pressure and kidney issues, and the various heart medications they've given him thus far have failed to strengthen his heart enough for him to bounce back any further. Time is now working against him, as week seven is presently upon us and a person's heart generally rebounds as much as it is going to by week eight after a heart attack.

Yesterday, the doctors alluded to the fact it will practically take a miracle for him to gain further ground and that they're running out of tricks to try on him. Good thing that in the Catholic faith, every day is a feast day of some sort, and with today being the feast of Our Lady of Lourdes and The World Day of Prayer for the Sick, I plan to beg the Lord and Our Lady for a supernatural cure.

Following Mass, I head to the hospital immediately, hurrying anxiously because visiting hours have begun and Bernie will be wondering why I'm late. Bernie's nurse, Michael, stops me in the hall before I enter his room. "Mr. Klein has been asking for you all morning. He wouldn't let me give him any pain medication this morning because he wanted to be alert when you arrived. There's something that he wants to say to you," he warns.

"Oh…okay," I say tentatively as I walk in to the room, thinking that this is very odd as Bernie asks constantly for his next dose of pain medicine because the pain all over his body is excruciating. "Good morning, honey, what's going on?" I ask as I kiss him multiple times on the forehead and face, a habit I learned from my highly affectionate mother-in-law, who grabs her loved ones faces with two hands and plants kisses all over them.

"Judy, please disconnect all of my life support and let me die!" he says with urgency in his voice. "I can't live like this anymore and I'm asking you to please let me die."

"What??!!!!" I react indignantly, feeling the impact of his words land like a sucker punch to my gut, taking my breath away. "Honey, you can't be serious! Do you have any idea how hard we've fought to save your life, and now you're asking me to let you die?!" I continue as I burst into tears and begin to sob uncontrollably.

"What's going on in here?" Michael asks, coming in to investigate why I'm crying so loudly. "What happened, Mrs. Klein?"

"My husband is telling me that he wants us to remove his life support and let him die," I tell him as I bawl openly. "We've spent two months trying to save his life and now he wants to die?" I demand, not expecting an answer.

"Mr. Klein," the nurse offers gently "it's very normal to feel depressed when you've been in the hospital for such a long time. But your wife and family want you to get well and come home with them. You've got to keep fighting to get well."

"I don't think I can fight anymore, Judy," Bernie says, looking up at me with a pitifully desperate look on his face. "I'm begging you, please disconnect everything and let me go," he says with resignation. "Michael, I'm ready for my pain medicine now."

"I'll talk to the doctor to see what he thinks," I say through tears as the nurse injects Bernie's IV line with painkillers. "You try to get some rest, okay?" He is sound asleep within minutes and I need to lie down and think, so I make my way to the built-in bed under the window where I shook with terror the night we arrived, knowing full well that Bernie has the legal right to make his own healthcare decisions now that he is alert and mentally competent, and that he can refuse life-saving medical treatment if he so chooses.

Further, I'm clear on the fact that my husband is not morally obligated to continue to avail himself of extraordinary means of support in order to stay alive. Pretty much everything we've done so far could be considered morally extraordinary, given how gravely ill he's been and how hard we've fought against the odds to save his life, especially in the beginning when the doctors predicted that he didn't have a reasonable chance of recovery.

Thinking back on the decisions I made to be as aggressive as possible with medical interventions, I'd do it all over again. I wasn't ready to let Bernie go then, and I'm much less ready now given the unexpected comeback of the "Miracle Man" from the brink of death. In spite of all of that, I know that I will have to respect Bernie's wishes if he is insistent, and that reality breaks open a dam of pent up grief that flows out of me like a river as I ponder the prospect of breaking the news to the children that their father has asked to be allowed to die.

I flip myself over and face toward the window, putting my back to the room to shield my face from the doctors and nurses who are coming in and out for rounds so they can't see the endless stream of tears running from my eyes. Of all of the scenarios I imagined concerning how and when Bernie would die, never in my wildest dreams did I envision his death being the result of disconnecting his life support at his own request. As far as I'm concerned, it would be a cruel joke if the doctors managed to save his life and get him awake and speaking so he could tell us to let him die. "Come on, God," I throw up a prayer in agony. "What am I supposed to do now?"

"Get up and bless the room with holy water," I hear a voice clearly speak to my spirit. "Take authority over the spirit of death," the voice commands me. Without hesitating, I roll over and jump to my feet, then find the bottle of holy water, which has the exorcism prayer prayed over it by a priest, sitting alongside a bag of relics and prayer cards on a tray next to Bernie's bed.

"I bless this room in the name of the Father, and of the Son and of the Holy Spirit," I say out loud as I sprinkle every inch of the room with the sacramental water that recalls our baptism into the death and resurrection of Christ. "In the name of Jesus, I command any spirit that is not of God to leave this room immediately," I continue with righteous determination as I proceed to Bernie's bed pouring the water into my hand to make the Sign of the Cross with it on his forehead. "I bless you in the name of the Father, and of the Son and of the Holy Spirit, and I take authority over the spirit of death and command you to be silent," I say assertively as Bernie sleeps soundly, praying the way I was taught over the years while attending various seminars on inner healing and deliverance.

Dr. Villandia walks in as I finish praying and I request a private conversation with him in the hall. After I convey that Bernie has asked for his life support to be disconnected, he assures me we're not at that point yet and that Bernie is probably suffering from depression. He promises to call the psychiatrist to have her adjust Bernie's medication for depression and to add an anti-anxiety drug as well.

"Dr. Villandia, what is the protocol for disconnecting someone's life support?" I query, sincerely wanting to understand how we will navigate that road if it becomes necessary. "How do we know when it's time to respect the patient's wishes to be allowed to die?" I continue. "How far do we push the envelope before we know that it's time to let nature to take its course?"

"Well, we don't disconnect a person's life support on their first request," he explains. "We try other remedies first like dealing with the depression and letting them talk to a mental health counselor. He's been through a lot and it's normal for someone in his condition to be depressed and anxious," he reassures me. "But, if he's insistent over a period of time that he wants his life support disconnected, then we'll have to honor his request," he says soberly in the Spanish accent that I still find familiar and consoling, even as we discuss this morbid subject. "At that point we would bring in the palliative care doctor to make sure he's comfortable and that he doesn't suffer any pain in the dying process."

"Okay, I understand," I respond, grateful for his knowledge and confidence. "And will you please let me know if we get to the point that we need to let him go?" I continue. "Doctor, I've made the decision all along to be as aggressive as possible with medical care because I really believed that's what Bernie would have wanted. But if he decides that's not what he wants, then we must honor that. I don't want this to become a science experiment where we're keeping him alive to see how far we can push it medically," I say sincerely, thinking that with the wonders of modern medicine, they could probably tweak his medications ad infinitum to keep him hanging onto the edge of life.

"You will know when we get to that point. It will be obvious if his body starts shutting down," he promises. "We still have a small window of opportunity to get him well. I have a new heart medication that I'm going to try and I'm hoping it will get him moving forward again," he says reassuringly as he grabs my hand and looks me in the eye. "Hang in there. I have a couple of tricks up my sleeve that we still haven't tried."

"Thank you, Dr. Villandia," I say wholeheartedly. "You have been a God-send and I'm so grateful for all you've done for Bernie."

With that, the doctor leaves and I find my cell phone to call my friend Johnnie, who is a powerful prayer warrior, to come to the hospital to pray for Bernie with me. Johnnie is available right after lunch, and when he arrives Bernie is sleeping soundly. After I explain to him that Bernie has asked that we remove his life support, we each assume a position on either side of his bed and anoint him with blessed oil to pray for his healing, laying a bag of relics on his chest, which includes relics of St. Pio of Pietrelcina, St. Francis of Assisi, St. Therese of Lisieux, Blessed Francis Xavier Seelos, and Blessed Anna Maria Taigi, a medieval mystic who also bore the stigmata on her body. Also in the bag is my personal Rosary, which has been blessed by Pope John Paul II and Pope Benedict XVI, along with the prayer card with the Novena to the Infant Jesus of Prague.

Johnnie begins to pray out loud, and I close my eyes and pray silently with both of my hands on Bernie's arm. As we pray, it strikes me like a lightning rod that Bernie has repeatedly stated for years that he is going to die before his sixty-fourth birthday, which he's three months shy of right now. His father died at sixty-four and Bernie has said to me so many times in recent years that he's going to die before he's sixty-four "just like my father did" that I've begun to admonish him to "stop saying that" every time it comes up, telling him that he shouldn't claim that for his life because it could become a self-fulfilling prophecy.

When there is a pause in Johnnie's prayers, I am prompted by the Holy Spirit to pray aloud, "In the name of Jesus Christ, I take authority over the spirit of death and any agreement Bernie has made with the spirit of death and I command you to leave right now and go to the foot of the Cross for disposition!" To my amazement, Bernie turns his head toward me and though he is in a deep slumber, lets out a loud growl-like grunt as I speak those words. He then turns his head back in the upright position facing the ceiling and continues to sleep peacefully. At this, I sprinkle Bernie's body with holy water and then pour some on his head, repeating the exact words I said before, with more authority this time. "In the name of Jesus Christ, I take authority over the spirit of death and any agreement Bernie made with the spirit of death and command you to leave right now and go to the foot of the Cross for disposition!" Again, Bernie turns his face directly toward me and lets out a deep growl as Johnnie and I watch a black shadow rise from his body and depart through the ceiling while Bernie continues to sleep. Though I am no exorcist and have historically been quite fearful when it comes to things involving dark spirits, there is no doubt in my mind that I just saw a spirit of death leave my husband's body. Johnnie and I lock eyes to acknowledge what we both saw, and I stand and praise God quietly as Johnnie says several other prayers.

"Wow, I think we've turned a corner," I say to Johnnie as I usher him into the hall minutes later.

"I think you're right," he says as he hugs me goodbye. "I'll bet you see a change in him after this," he continues. "Call me if you need me to come back and pray again."

The afternoon is fairly quiet with Bernie sleeping much of the time and with Renee showing up with a large bag from Whole Foods that includes all-natural "Stress Remedy" lozenges, prompted by Jo Jo's report to her of my weepy behavior this morning. The bag also includes soups, salads, fruit and bread, as I've lost fifteen pounds now and my sisters have begun to make it their job to keep me supplied with nourishing food to eat. I manage to enjoy a nice, long nap after sucking on a few "Stress Remedy" lozenges, and then I write an update to ask our family and friends to step up the prayers.

Bernie Update: Wednesday, Feb. 11
Feast of Our Lady of Lourdes

Dear Friends:

A friend wrote yesterday to ask if "no news is good news." Yes and no. Bernie had a setback on Sunday night (fluid around his heart and lungs) and had to go back on the ventilator all day Monday. The good news is that they took him off the ventilator Tuesday and he has been breathing on his own since. The bad news is that the doctor told us it would take him a week to recover from that one day setback, so he has spent all week trying to get back to where he was last week. He has been weak with very low blood pressure since the setback. The blood pressure is low because his heart function is poor, and if the heart is too weak to pump, the kidneys will remain shut down. It appears he is in somewhat of a "Catch 22" —his heart remains too weak to support the blood pressure and kidney function that are necessary to get better.

As I shared in a previous update, Bernie's progress last week was remarkable. We were talking about a move to a rehab center, but he "crashed" on Sunday night (something that happens with a lot of heart patients after a push forward). We are both disappointed and his spirits have been pretty low. The next week will tell us what his heart is going to do insofar as recovering function, as the heart usually recovers as much as it is going to by six to eight weeks after a heart attack. We are on week seven and quite frankly, it will take a miracle for him to get the boost forward that he needs to recover any further. The conversations with the medical personnel have been discouraging these last few days, so I am doing what I know to do—asking for more prayers.

We have had many miracles so far, including him surviving the initial insult to his heart, which generally kills people in "three minutes" according to Dr. Madden. He then went on to beat the odds of surviving the first few days at Ochsner, where he arrived in total organ failure, and as one nurse put it recently, "basically dead." He woke up, got off the ventilator and is neurologically intact—all against tremendous odds and against the predictions of the doctors. I have learned that they cannot

114

predict what God is going to do. Nor can they predict how prayer can change the course of events in a situation.

I am asking you, my friends and prayer warriors, to pray for another miracle—the miracle that Bernie's heart will recover enough to sustain his blood pressure and jump-start some kidney function. I continue to surrender him to the Lord and am praying for God's will to be done. The Lord tells us to ASK Him for what we want—we want Bernie to get well and come home with us and we are asking the Lord for that specifically. Your fervent and continued prayers are greatly appreciated.

Love and blessings to all,

Judy

PS-This shouldn't be a PS, as it is important, but Bernie has repeatedly stated that he saw Jesus. He told both Kara and me that they spoke, but not in a language that we use on earth. He has told me several times that it was a "vision" that he cannot articulate. God has done great things already. I praise Him and give him glory for all!

February 12, 2009

Morning comes again and I awaken and hurry to the hospital so I can be there when visiting hours begin, knowing that sitting alone in his room lends itself to Bernie's depression. Happily, I find him brighter and stronger today, and I'm pleasantly surprised to find him smiling and in a good humor as I kiss him good morning.

Dr. Villandia's wonderful spicy cologne in the hall announces his presence for rounds and he enters the room with his usual greeting, "Buenos Dias, Bernardo! Como estas?"

Without hesitating, Bernie answers very enthusiastically, "Great!!"

"Great?" I respond in a surprised tone as the doctor and I flank his bed on either side, taking note of the dramatic change in him since yesterday when he asked to have his life support disconnected. "That is music to my ears! Why are you feeling so great?"

"I don't know…this is the best I've felt since I got here. I can feel my strength returning and I am getting better," Bernie offers with a visibly different countenance and attitude than the previous morning.

"Wow!" I say thankfully. "Praise God. I'm so happy to hear that."

"Me too," Dr. Villandia interjects. "And your new heart medication will hopefully make you feel even better. I ordered the nurses to begin it just now. Let's pray that it gets your heart stronger so we can move you to a rehab center soon." After a brief check up and assessment of Bernie's hand, foot and back wounds, which are not healing due to the fact that his circulation is so poor, the doctor departs and I pull my chair up beside the bed to begin morning prayers.

"Do you want to hear about my near death experience?" Bernie asks unexpectedly and unassumingly as I sit down.

"Oh my gosh…yes!!!" I say excitedly. "I've been waiting forever for you to tell me this! What did Jesus say to you?" I want to know.

"Judy, I died and I remember it clearly," he begins slowly and quietly. "I saw my spirit leave my body and I could see myself floating in the air, looking down at my body, where I could see my damaged heart. It

116

looked like my heart was torn in half and one side was a vivid color of blue that looked like ugly debris—and I knew it represented all of the things I had done in my life that were not pleasing to God. The other side was a beautiful gold—and I knew it represented all of the things I had done that were pleasing to God," he continues with a soft, intentional voice that seeps a sacred silence.

"I could feel myself being pulled over and over toward the blue side of my heart, even though I wanted to go toward the gold side. I felt that I had to make a choice, but I felt a strong emotional struggle over which side to choose. Finally, I chose the gold and started moving toward the gold side of my heart and, when I did, I got on a gold bus and went toward the light. I followed the light all of the way to heaven. And, Judy," he continues with deadly seriousness, "When I got there, I wasn't permitted to enter."

"You weren't permitted to enter?" I ask quizzically, mindful of the man who previously maintained that he was certain he would go to heaven because he was a "good person."

"No, I wasn't permitted to enter. All of the sudden, I started going toward the dark side of my heart again and I started heading toward the darkness, and when I did, I met the most unimaginable creatures," Bernie relays somberly. "They were indescribably hideous and they had tusks coming out of the center of their heads. You know what tusks are?" he asks as though it's the first time I've ever heard of the concept. "And these creatures began to assault me and violate my body, beating me up and ramming things down my throat and into the other orifices of my body. I was begging them to stop, but they just kept beating me and screaming in my ears with hideous voices yelling, 'We're here to help you!! We're here to help you!' I was pleading with them, saying, "Please...please, I beg you, this isn't the kind of help I need."

"How did you resolve it?" I ask, spellbound at his story, especially as it comes forth from a man who never believed in demons and insisted for years that I was "too focused on the demonic" when I would speak of Satan and his minions.

"I surrendered to God," he says slowly and deliberately, emphasizing each word purposefully. "And when I did, I was given food, air and water— and I had so much peace. I was told by God to go back— that I needed to make amends with God, my life and the people in my life. And, Judy," he says, looking me right in the eye after a moment's hesitation, "this is my purification. And I NEED it," he continues, conveying his experience with a level of honesty and humility that I have rarely seen in my husband in the twenty-four years I've known him.

The word "purification" is not something I've ever heard leave my husband's lips, but it's a term I'm well acquainted with from Catholic theology. The idea around purification is that in order to go to heaven we must be objectively holy, and the bible is explicit that "nothing unholy will enter heaven." (Rev. 21:27) In order to become holy, we must be sanctified—made holy—either in this life or the next. Purification happens in this life when we embrace Jesus Christ through faith and baptism, and then die to ourselves as we strive to live according to Christ's teachings. Purification is an ongoing process as we allow our faith—and our suffering—to have a transformative effect on us. When we do, we become pliable, teachable and moldable as we allow ourselves to be conformed to Christ, and as we let the "fire" of God's love change us into a more accurate image and likeness of Him, burning away the dross in us—or as Bernie called it, "ugly debris"—that is incompatible with the love of God.

If we still need purification when we depart this life, it's known as "purgatory," which Pope John Paul II said is not so much a "place" as it is an experience of being cleansed as we see the truth about ourselves—which is often very painful—in the blazing fire of God's love as we enter heaven. Apparently, Bernie has had this experience of truth, and it's clear to him that he stands in need of this time of cleansing.

"Judy," Bernie continues with his story, "I've had that vision in my mind continuously for weeks and it's all I've been able to see every time I close my eyes. But I've been unable to speak about it until now," he continues. "Something changed yesterday...I don't know what it was."

"Wow!!!! That is incredible!" I respond in stunned amazement, suspecting that I know exactly what caused the change. "Do you know what happened yesterday? After you asked me to let you die, I started praying and I heard God say to take authority over a spirit of death. I called Johnnie Hernandez to come pray with me and while we were praying over you, it occurred to me that you had made an agreement with the spirit of death by insisting that you were going to die before you turn sixty-four—almost like putting a curse on yourself," I continue as Bernie looks up at me with wide eyes. "Johnnie and I took authority over that spirit and we watched it leave your body. And you are completely different today," I convey with awe, as the change in him is truly remarkable.

"Well, I didn't know that happened, but I know that something changed," Bernie agrees with a smile. "And you know what, Judy? Every time I close my eyes now all I can see is the Sacred Heart of Jesus."

"Praise God!!!" I enthusiastically reply. "You didn't know what happened because you were asleep when we prayed. But there's no doubt in my mind that I saw a spirit of death leave your body. Johnnie and I both saw it."

"Thank you for praying for me," Bernie responds as he looks up at me with sincere gratitude in his eyes. "And thank you for being by my side all of this time in this hospital. I finally understand how much you love me," he continues gratefully.

His words pierce my heart to the core because no matter how many times I've told Bernie that I love him, I've sensed that he's never really believed it deep down. And the truth is, though I've loved my husband like crazy since the day we met, my fear and resentment over his addiction to chaos and his propensity for aggressive and reckless behavior have kept a distance between us that we have both always felt.

Additionally, our marriage has been loaded with high drama and high passion, and we've vacillated constantly between being friends, companions and lovers to behaving like little children in a sandbox, throwing sand into each other's eyes. Woefully, while Bernie and I experienced many moments of friendship and camaraderie, we have just as often done deep damage to each other by using our words and actions rashly and ragingly to tear each other to pieces instead of to bless and build each other up, keeping trust from ever taking deep root.

I've had plenty of time to think about all of that during these extended two months, as I've sat silently beside Bernie's sickbed for countless insufferable hours, wondering if he would live. During that time, I've engaged in hard reflection on the shortcomings in our marriage, especially on my own sins and weaknesses, which have hung on my heart like a heavy weight ever since Bernie's heart began to fail. While Bernie was having his come-to-Jesus, I was experiencing my own illumination about the ways I could have been kinder, more loving and more appreciative toward my spouse. It has occurred to me many times that this is *my* God-given opportunity to learn to love unconditionally, and that I've needed to learn the lesson of giving for the sake of love itself, not because I expected to get something in return.

In a moment in Bernie's life when he's too sick to give anything back, I'm convicted that I've been given the great gift of having the opportunity to lavish him with love, and I'm aware that is part of *my* miracle. I've kissed his face a thousand times praying that somehow my time with him here will help repair the hurt that I caused through my iniquities and failures to love, including my constant criticism that drove him to say in exasperation "I just can't do anything right in your eyes!" every time I would present my bevy of complaints about him.

"You are very welcome, honey," I respond tearfully to Bernie's expression of gratitude and acknowledgement of my love for him. "I do love you very, very much and there is no place on this earth I would rather be than next to you right now," I add honestly. "Can you please forgive me for the unkind ways I've treated you?" I ask.

"Sure baby," Bernie says solemnly, "if you'll forgive me for treating you like a piece of crap for twenty-four years."

"I do forgive you," I offer.

"Thank you, baby," Bernie continues humbly before shifting gears. "Judy, when I get out of here I've got to tell people this story, because people need to understand how much God loves them. I finally get it—God loves us SO much," he continues with conviction and certainty, because despite seeing his own demons, Bernie's overarching experience of being in the presence of God was one of unfathomable love.

"Look, my whole life has been about making a deal—it's been about making money. Now I understand that none of that is important. None of that means anything," Bernie discloses definitively. "I don't know what I'm going to do when I get out of here, but there are two things that I do know. I have a mission from God to tell people how much He loves them. And I will never work for money again," he continues as I stand beside him with my mouth practically agape as he shares his story of the illumination of his heart and soul in the light of God's love, reminding me somewhat of St. Thomas Aquinas' famous conclusion after a profound revelation of God during prayer one day that forced him to put down his pen forever. In the light of God's unspeakable love, the theological and philosophical genius said, "All that I have written seems to me so much straw after the things that have been revealed to me."

Though Bernie's time has been spent primarily trying to make money instead of writing inspired theological treatises, his understanding that it was all "straw" in the light of what he has seen leads him to say, "I don't know how I'm going to support our family in the future, but I know I won't work for money. I never understood what Kara meant when she used to tell me that God would take care of everything for her when I pressured her to pursue her singing career more aggressively. She would tell me that it was a ministry—not a career—and that she was going to pray and trust God because He would work it all out," he continues. "Although I thought it was ridiculous at the time, I understand for the first time in my life what that means. God will take care of everything and I know that now. I have so much peace. I have SO MUCH PEACE," he says with added emphasis as he closes his eyes and begins to fade.

After he falls asleep, I sit beside his bed in wonder, pondering the majesty of our Father in heaven's mercy and love. I consider the incredible trajectory of supernatural events since Bernie had his heart attack eight weeks ago, when he first he told me that he was praying the Memorare day and night, and that the Immaculate Heart of Mary was before him every time he closed his eyes. He then went into organ failure and had a near death experience where he saw the condition of his own heart, as well as his own unworthiness for heaven and the demons that had a hold on his life. Now he's in the presence of the Sacred Heart of Jesus, which is the incarnational symbol of God's inexhaustible love and mercy for mankind, experienced in a personal and concrete way through an intimate love relationship with Jesus—who extends His heart to each of us asking only that we receive and trust His great love for us. I am bowled over by what God has done and awed by His presence with us.

"Wow!" is all I can pray over and over again as I ponder the one spiritual devotion that Bernie had of praying the Memorare daily, remembering its words to Our Lady that "never was it known that anyone who fled to your protection, implored your help or sought your intercession was left unaided." It is patently evident to me once again that Mary can only lead us to her son Jesus, the Word of God who became Incarnate through her own flesh and blood. As much as I struggled with the devotion that Catholics have to the Blessed Mother when I reverted from Protestantism, Bernie's profound conversion is yet another dramatic instance of Mary pointing one of her children to Jesus. It is stunning to me what has transpired here, as Bernie has not only been given a "new heart and a new spirit" as God promises in Ezekiel 36, but the gifts of the Immaculate and Sacred Hearts to boot!

The Blessed Mother's words to me from 1988, when I heard her speak in the darkness of the night saying: "I will cleanse your family" are ringing in my ears as I try to take in the profundity of this miracle and how it fits into what God has been doing in our lives for years. What my husband just shared with me is much more than I have hoped for or imagined as I've prayed for his conversion for many long years, and my faith is bolstered once again as God continues to move miraculously in our midst.

I call my sister-in-law Hedy to tell her what has transpired and that she must come to the hospital to talk to Bernie.

"Hedy," I begin excitedly "Bernie has finally told me about his near death experience! You have to come over here and talk to him!"

"I'm on my way to the hospital to visit right now," she responds. "Can you tell me what happened?"

"No," I continue, "you need to hear this from him first-hand. All I can say is that what he just shared with me is incredible! Do you remember the Blessed Mother's prophecy when I came back to the Church when she said: 'I will cleanse your family?' Well, that prophecy is being fulfilled in your brother Bernard. I am completely blown away!"

"Oh my gosh! Thank you, Jesus!" Hedy exclaims. "I'll be there in an hour. I can't wait to hear this!"

When Hedy arrives an hour later, she rushes into the room to speak to Bernie, who is lying awake very serenely in his bed with a calm smile on his face. His countenance is visibly different from the pained expression he's borne on his face through the many weeks of suffering he has endured while both unconscious and conscious.

"Wow, Bernie, you look great!" is the first thing out of Hedy's mouth as she kisses her brother hello.

"I feel great," he responds with a knowing smile.

"Bernie, have you been to the other side?" Hedy launches right in.

He closes his eyes then opens them purposefully while nodding his head yes.

"Did you see my dad?" Hedy continues using their typical family expression of saying "my mother" or "my dad" whenever they refer to their parents, which is a literal translation from their native Spanish.

Bernie quietly nods no, without giving up any information.

"Should I fast for you?" she persists.

At this, Bernie smiles broadly and speaks. "It's okay...I want to thank you."

"You want to thank me? For what?" she asks perplexed.

"Because you got it right," he continues, referring to the strong torch of faith Hedy has carried for our family and to her conviction that she must evangelize others, which she has done by having numerous retreats, Masses, and Rosary groups over the years.

"I want to work with you. Time is short and we don't have time to waste," Bernie says next. "Hedy, Jesus is so good. He has work for us to do," he continues as I stand on the other side of the bed watching Hedy's transition from interested excitement to open weeping as she, too, sees the visible, tangible answer to so many prayers coming to fruition before her eyes. He then shares with her his experience of seeing his heart, of meeting God and of the great sense of love he experienced in His presence, equating it to his sixtieth birthday party at Hedy's house when the entire family went around the table affirming what we specifically loved and appreciated about Bernie.

"That night at your house...that's a good example of the love God has for us," Bernie continues quietly. "I love you, Hedy. You have a good heart," he concludes as he turns to me and says, "Judy, we need to do it like Hedy. She gets it."

As I watch my sister-in-law sobbing, I understand how monumental these comments are to her, because I know full well how negative and belittling Bernie was for so many years about Hedy and her events, which generally included a pressing call to conversion and the strong admonition to pray the Rosary daily, as Our Lady has instructed in so many apparitions around the world.

"I'm going to start calling her 'Chicken Little'," he used to say in his typical sarcastic humor "because every time you talk to her, she insists the sky is falling! She's such an idiot! I can't stand stupidity!" he would say with exasperation.

There is no hint of that sarcasm now, only gratitude, understanding and humility, as the former mocker has become a believer, not through human persuasion, but through the supernatural intervention of God Himself. Hedy and I exchange tearfully giddy goodbyes in the hallway, shaking our heads in wonder at our new Bernard.

"I told you that you had to see it for yourself," I giggle as I hug her goodbye. "God is amazing, isn't he?"

A short time later, Dr. Villandia arrives and is so surprised by the change in Bernie that he decides to call the physical therapist in to sit Bernie up on the side of the bed. He sustains twenty minutes of sitting with the physical therapist holding him up, and though it is very painful physically, it's a giant leap forward in Bernie's recovery process that I memorialize by taking a picture on my cell phone. Dr. Villandia instructs the physical therapist to take him out of bed completely tomorrow and writes an order for a cardiac chair to be sent to his room immediately for the therapist to sit him in, which will be another significant step in the lengthy undertaking of getting Bernie better.

As the day progresses, Bernie asks me five different times to do his physical therapy exercises with him, which the physical therapist has taught me how to do so we can expedite the process of strengthening Bernie's muscles. The mood is peaceful and light in his room, and Bernie shares with me during a quiet moment when I ask him what he's thinking that he is simply enjoying "fellowship with God." I'm certain that we've turned a corner in his recovery and fully convinced that Bernie will get well now. I will begin looking at rehabilitation centers tomorrow so we can take the next step forward.

Late in the day we receive an e-mail from a friend and client of Bernie's sharing a dream she had of him. I read it to Bernie, as I have been doing with many of the e-mails that arrive lately, including him in the dialogue of prayer and love that has enveloped us in his illness.

Dear Judy,

I don't ever dream much... But last night you & Bernie came to my home. He looked wonderful... thin... but our Bernie fully intact. I am

hoping this is a sign that our Bernie is coming back. He was so happy...
We were all happy! I am saying a rosary often just for Bernie.

All my love & many prayers,

Kim

In his typical humorous style, Bernie dictates a response:

Dear Kim,

Thanks for the email. I hope your dreams come true.

Love,

Bernie (dictated by Bernie)

We end the day by watching "My Cousin Vinnie" together, the hysterically funny comedy in which Joe Pesci stars as an attorney from the Bronx who comes to a small southern town to defend his cousin from a murder charge. It has long been Bernie's favorite movie and even made him drool on his shirt once because he laughed so hard while watching it. Though he only cracks a faint smile at the film now, it helps to pass the time, bringing a sliver of normalcy back into our lives as we await the future.

February 19, 2009

The past week has brought much more physical therapy, and this morning begins with an aggressive attempt by the physical therapist to keep Bernie in an upright position for a sustained period of time, which she accomplishes by strapping him into a cardiac chair for forty long, arduous minutes. He's still immobile from the neck down, notwithstanding a small range of motion in his hands and feet, but since putting him in a sitting position is supposed to help strengthen his core and the other muscles in his body so he will become capable of moving them too, Bernie's all for it. He's completely wiped out when it's over with, but we're both happy that he's crossed another hurdle.

Following physical therapy, a technician comes in to perform an ultrasound on Bernie's heart to determine how much heart function he's regained at this point. The report is extremely disappointing, because it shows that he hasn't gained the slightest bit of ground since the December 26 ultrasound that showed that only 25% of his heart was working, meaning that 75% of his heart—including the entire left ventricle—is completely non-functional. I am perplexed as to why it's taken this long to look at Bernie's heart via ultrasound, but in spite of the report, I'm planning to go look at rehab centers this afternoon, as I'm anxious to get Bernie to a facility that can accommodate more aggressive rehabilitation of his body to strengthen him toward recovery. In addition to the ultrasound, the doctor has ordered a swallow test to see if Bernie can begin eating solid food or if it will cause him to aspirate, which happens when food or liquid enters the lungs, resulting in pneumonia and other very dangerous health conditions. Again, very disappointing news comes our way when Bernie fails the swallow test.

"He just needs more time to heal," I think as I make my way toward the elevator to get some soup in the cafeteria for lunch. As I am walking through the lobby, the nurse who serves as an assistant to Drs. Meiser and Villandia stops me. "Mrs. Klein, I've been looking for you. I need to speak to you about your husband," Nurse Lipscomb states kindly, but matter-of-factly.

"Oh, I was just heading downstairs to get some lunch. Did you hear that he sat in a cardiac chair for forty minutes this morning?" I ask, assuming she heard the good news.

126

"No, I'm here to talk to you about his ultrasound and swallow test," she continues pointedly. "I need to let you know that your husband is not going to get any better than he is right now, no matter what we do."

"What???!!!" I react with complete surprise, finding myself bumping up against my denial once again, as I have apparently moved again from hope to what Dr. Villandia calls "stupidity" in the past week. "What do you mean that he's not going to get any better? He sat in a chair for forty minutes today. And I've been instructed to start looking at rehab centers to move him to," I persist.

"Mrs. Klein, I'm sorry to tell you this, but in the twenty years I've been working with heart patients, I've never seen anyone who is as sick as your husband improve after six to eight weeks. His heart is too damaged for him to get any better, and he's too sick for a heart transplant. He's as well as he's going to get, and he's crossed the threshold of time during which he could possibly improve."

"Are you serious?" I ask in disbelief, feeling my throat lock as I attempt to swallow her words. "You mean to tell me that he's never going to regain any more heart function than he has right now? And that he'll never be able to move from the neck down for the rest of his life?" I continue in an alarmed voice, because in spite of the ultrasound report which clearly shows that Bernie has not gained any ground in recovering heart function since before Christmas, I'm somehow still hoping and believing he can get better.

"Yes, that's correct," she states unwaveringly.

"Does the doctor know you're telling me this?" is all I can think to ask next, referring to Dr. Meiser, who's back on hospital duty as of this week.

"Yes, he asked me to communicate this to you. I'm sorry," she proceeds, as she gives me a hug and walks off. I'm too dumbfounded to ask her what we're supposed to do now in light of this information, and I stand in the hall not knowing which direction to take because my appetite just crashed, and there's no need to go to the cafeteria anymore. I can't go back to Bernie's room as he'll see how upset I am, so I sit on the sofa by the elevator with my mind racing as I try to assimilate this dismal information. Minutes later, my phone rings indicating that my mother is calling. I answer the phone and burst into tears, conveying to her what Nurse Lipscomb just told me.

"Judy, I'm at Commander's Palace having a lunch meeting with Ron Diliberti, whom you met when we were all in New York last Christmas for Kara's concert. I was telling him about Bernie and he said that we have one of the most renowned cardiologists in the world locally at University Hospital, and he'd be glad to make a few phone calls to see if this doctor would be willing to give you another opinion about Bernie."

"Who could he possibly call, Mom?" I wonder numbly. "You know that University doctors don't have privileges to come into Ochsner and, besides, no one is going want to touch Bernie with a ten-foot-pole two months into this."

"Well, Ron is friends with Nancy Pelosi, and he can call her cell phone right now and see if she can get the doctor to come assess Bernie's situation. She has a connection to him somehow and at least he could come give you his opinion," my mother presses on in her typical manner which has earned her the reputation over the years of "never taking no for an answer."

"Sure, Mom," I concede, feeling the walls closing in around us as our options seem to be running out. "What do we have to lose at this point? I guess we could use another opinion here." And with that nod yes, helped along by the Minority Leader of the House of Representatives, the ball starts rolling to bring Dr. Pierre LeCroix, head of cardiology at University Hospital, into the halls of Ochsner to tell us what he thinks about Bernie.

Fortified by a tiny wave of hope, I head to Bernie's room to tell him that a new doctor is coming on board to assess his condition, trying to figure out as I walk down the hall how to spin this positively so Bernie won't become alarmed. Dr. Meiser is in his room when I arrive, looking to give Bernie and me the results of his ultrasound. As Bernie is asleep, I take the opportunity to tell Dr. Meiser what his nurse disclosed to me in the hall, hoping he'll say she was totally off base and out of line to say that there's no hope for my husband. Instead, he looks at me with an embarrassed grin, laughing slightly as he says, "Oh, yes. Nurse Libscomb. They call her the 'angel of death' because she's sent to break the news to the families when there's nothing else we can do."

"Right," I say as my blood boils in my veins over Dr. Meiser's lack of grace and sensitivity. I clench my teeth and shake his hand sharply as he prepares to leave the room, thinking to myself that I don't give a darn how offended he's going to be when I bring Dr. Pierre LeCroix into this hospital to give me a second opinion about his patient. I want to speak to Dr. Villandia, and have already made it known that I would prefer for him to stay on the case the entire time, but he's at the clinic and won't be back in the hospital for another two weeks. Though I've objected to this arrangement of switching doctors every two weeks, it's how things are done here and I'm impotent to change their firmly established practice of alternating turns in the clinic and the hospital.

Before long, Bernie wakes up and I begin to navigate the discussion with him about the ultrasound results, the condition of his heart, and the fact that I am trying to get a cardiologist from University to come here to give us a second opinion about his prospects for recovery. He is agreeable to having Dr. LeCroix come in, and within an hour my phone rings and I'm on the line with a stranger whose thick French accent makes Dr. Villandia's Honduran accent seem mild.

"Mrs. Klein," he launches in "this is Dr. Pierre LeCroix from University Hospital. I received a call from Nancy Pelosi's office asking me to come assess your husband, whom I understand is a heart patient there."

"Yes, Dr. LeCroix," I respond gratefully. "The doctors here are telling us there is nothing else they can do for him. I've spoken to my husband about it, and we're so thankful that you're willing to come give us your opinion. We could really use some advice at this point."

"Okay. I'm trying to obtain clearance from the hospital to come into his room and, as soon as I do, I'll let you know," he adds before he hangs up.

It doesn't take long for LeCroix to accomplish his mission and call back to confirm that he'll be here by four o'clock this afternoon. There is a hushed uproar among the hospital personnel once the word hits the floor that a University cardiologist will be coming here to evaluate Bernie, and while I'm concerned about offending the staff, that is the least of my worries at the moment. The day ticks on and at long last I'm informed that Dr. LeCroix has arrived, and as I stand outside Bernie's room waiting for him, I can sense the tension in the hall as the kind Frenchman makes his way toward us in his white University lab coat. He introduces himself and enters Bernie's room, but not before covering himself from head to toe with a protective gown, facial mask and gloves that insulate a doctor from possible contamination that he could carry to other patients. Dr. LeCroix seems surprised by Bernie's condition at first glance, especially by the gangrenous state of his fingers and toes, as they are now irreversibly black from the extended use of the blood pressure medication he's been on for so long. The doctor examines Bernie slowly and methodically, asking various questions as he goes.

After inspecting him thoroughly from head to toe, Dr. LeCroix turns to me and says, "Mrs. Klein, your husband is septic. He has a blood infection and he cannot get better if it's not treated very aggressively. We'll be happy to take him at University, and our infectious disease specialists will be very assertive about getting this infection under control. If you'd like, you can come to the hospital in the morning and I'll give you a tour of the facility. If you're comfortable with what we can offer, I'll send an ambulance to pick Mr. Klein up tomorrow afternoon," Dr. LeCroix graciously offers. With that, he bids us goodbye and exits the room.

Bernie and I lock eyes, as I say, "Honey, it's up to you. Do you want me to go look at University tomorrow?"

"Yes, Judy, I want to go to University," he responds with certainty. "I want to go where my son was," he continues.

I've been somewhat hesitant since the name of University Hospital first came up, knowing that's where Marshall passed away four-and-a-half years ago. My fear is that Bernie will go there to die where his son died, and that thought is more than a little disconcerting to me. Nevertheless, it's what Bernie wants, and I will honor his request to investigate having him transferred there.

I call Renee to ask her to come with me tomorrow, and we arrange to meet first thing in the morning. The day grinds on slowly, and I can feel the tension as we stand again on the narrow rope between dread and hope, not knowing what tomorrow will bring. Bernie and I burn up the time by talking continuously whenever he is awake, re-visiting many of the events in our life together. He is frail and weak, but he's mentally and emotionally astute.

We talk about how I knew I would marry him the first time we ever spoke during that memorable phone call when I was looking for a job after my stint at the World's Fair ended. He had recently opened his public relations and advertising firm in New Orleans, and I came to his office for an interview a few days after we spoke on the phone. It was love at first sight when we saw each other, and I was completely taken by his charisma and enthusiasm. We reminisce about the days our children were born and

130

about many of the happy times we had together in our marriage. We also talk about the ways we hurt each other and about the endless, frustrating power struggle that went on in our marriage, asking one another's forgiveness again for the offenses we committed over the years, which were many. It is a precious time of healing and transparency and I'm conscious of the fact that that this dialogue is part of our miracle, too, even as Dr. Madden's words ring in my ears that Bernie "should have died in three minutes" from the initial insult to his heart on December 23.

I can't help thinking about the regret I would have had if I had never been able to speak to my husband again, and I am inexpressibly grateful that we have this time to share and to make amends with each other and unload some of the burdens of the past from our hearts. His soul has been illuminated, as has mine. He has seen what's important and what lasts, and I've been graced with that vision, too. We do not know what the future holds, but today we've been given the chance to mend the threads of love, and weave something new into the tapestry of our lives by loving one another openly and unconditionally, and we're taking advantage of every waking moment to do just that.

February 20, 2009

Renee and I meet out front of the hospital on University Avenue and navigate our way back to the Administrative Offices of University Hospital looking for Dr. LeCroix. The hospital sits in the middle of a rather seedy, dangerous part of New Orleans, directly adjacent to what used to be the old Charity Hospital in pre-Katrina days, where Renee was a Recovery Room nurse for years in the late seventies and early eighties. She had plenty of war stories to tell in those days—stories that generally coincided with the six o'clock news broadcast relating the drama of the latest shooting or accident victims in the city, many of whom she cared for in post-surgery recovery. I used to drop her off at work on the street where we just parked, then watch as she made her way into what seemed to me to be a high-intensity, high-risk work environment. The hospital drew not only the city's poor, but also the criminal element that had been involved in the latest robberies and drug deals gone bad. Eventually, it got to be too much for her and she went on to get a degree in hospital administration, working at Touro Hospital for several years before she got married and had four children. After a divorce and Hurricane Katrina, she left the health care field altogether for a career as a building contractor, passing the very difficult contractor's licensing exam on her first try.

Before long, we find Dr. LeCroix, who greets us warmly and offers to begin our tour. We make our way up to the third floor Cardiac Intensive Care Unit, which is full of critically ill patients who are at some point in the process of recovering from heart attacks or heart surgery, much like Bernie. We then walk to the opposite end of the facility and take the elevator to the fourth floor post-surgery ICU, which is brimming with high-level activity as the nurses there administer hands-on attention to a wing full of post-operative patients who are in need of intensive care. As we enter the hall with its dozen or so glassed-in rooms, I feel a chill go through my body as I have flashback of being in this place four years ago the morning Marshall's life support was disconnected. I'm certain that we just passed the room where Marshall died, which is situated at the beginning of the hall directly across from the nurse's station. I vividly remember the nurses weeping openly at our family tragedy as they tried to work and care for patients that dreadful morning. I fight back fear and sorrow as Dr. LeCroix escorts us to the glassed-in cubicle at the dead end of the hall on the left, telling us that he will more than likely put Bernie here, because the nursing care is more aggressive in this unit and because the room at the end will afford us more privacy. He's trying to work out the details of making it available to Bernie right away if we're interested in transferring him here.

Renee and I are both quite impressed with personal attention we've received thus far and, when the tour ends, we bid Dr. LeCroix goodbye and assure him we'll have a decision as soon as I can get back to Ochsner to discuss things with Bernie. My sister and I then stand in front of the hospital weighing the positives and negatives of transferring Bernie here. It seems like a good idea to both of us to get a new set of eyes and hands on his case, but moving him could involve very serious risks, as his condition is still very critical. I am also wary of bringing him to the floor where Marshall died, and it seems too strange a coincidence that we would wind up within yards of where his eldest son's life expired. My head is whirling when I get in the car, and I decide to call Marshall's wife Lisa to verify whether he indeed died on the fourth floor of the hospital. "Yep, that's right," she tells me without hesitation. "I'll never forget it. The memory is forever seared into my mind and I remember it like it was yesterday."

Bernie is anxiously awaiting a report when I arrive back at Ochsner, and I am open and honest with him about what took place there. "I think they will be very assertive about treating you there, Bernie," I begin "and I don't think there's anything else they can do for you here. But they want to move you to the floor where Marshall died, and I have to tell you, that scares the heck out of me," I continue as I take his hand and sit beside the bed. "Also, you are very weak and the doctors here have warned us you might not survive the transfer. They haven't even wanted to take you out of your room to have an MRI done. It will take a toll on you to move you to another hospital."

"Judy," he says with earnest pleading in his eyes, "I want to go where my son was. Please transfer me to University."

"Okay, honey," I acquiesce. "If that's what you want to do, I'll set it up right away." I immediately call Dr. LeCroix to give him our decision, and the wheels start turning to move Bernie to University. I'm told it will take several hours to complete the discharge, as he's been in the CICU for over two months and the paperwork trail on his case is enormous. There is tension in the air among the staff about our departure, but I use the time to say goodbye to and thank the many nurses on the floor who have cared for Bernie day in and day out, especially a beautiful African-American nurse named Priscilla who has given Bernie and me numerous pep talks about keeping our eyes firmly on Jesus during this long ordeal. She has been exceedingly kind to us, and even went so far as to instruct me to bring Bernie's electric razor to the hospital, whereupon she proceeded to give him an hour-long shave with great tenderness and attention to detail, "so he could feel like himself again." I was delighted when she finished, as I could see again the face of the man I fell in love with after she removed the long, white beard he had grown while he was flat on his back. She shaved his face regularly after that. Another day she gave me a long massage because it was obvious I was exhausted and down, telling me as she rubbed my neck and shoulders, "Baby, I've been praying for you day and night because I can see that you're carrying a lot on your shoulders."

Priscilla has also been vigilant about closing the curtains and guarding the door for several hours a day while on duty to keep the traffic and chaos out of the room so we can get some rest. "Mr. Klein needs to sleep and so do you," she'd say firmly. "The body cannot heal when a person does not get enough sleep and they wake you up every fifteen minutes in the hospital. But nobody is coming in this room for the next two hours without getting past me!" she would declare protectively. Bernie and I have both grown to love this kind woman, and I rue the thought of not having her comforting presence as we move forward to an unfamiliar place.

The day is long and emotional as I disassemble the pictures, posters and banners from the walls and pack everything we've accumulated over many weeks to haul it to the car. Once the discharge papers are signed, it takes several more hours for the ambulance to arrive for the transfer. Finally, around 9:00 p.m. two EMTs appear on the floor and, without much fanfare, they clumsily disconnect the bags of medicine that have been sustaining Bernie's life, leaving him with a bare minimum of medication on board for the transfer. I walk alongside his stretcher and take the elevator down to the lobby with the transfer crew, wondering if Bernie will make it to University alive. As we exit through the hospital's large glass doors, I'm thinking of how ironic it is that Bernie and I are indeed "walking out of here together" as I've said many times we would do, while knowing this is not at all what I envisioned when I spoke those words. The good news is that Bernie is still alive, and as my mother keeps telling me, "Where there's life, there's hope."

We drive off into the dark of the night, and I follow closely behind the ambulance as it proceeds down Jefferson Highway to Claiborne Avenue, then down Claiborne to the Superdome, where we are halted by bumper-to-bumper Mardi Gras traffic. We sit dead in traffic for a minute before the ambulance turns on its lights and siren to push through the gridlock. I try my best to stay on its bumper, praying all the while that Bernie hangs in there. My heart begins to race as I lose the vehicle in the thickly crowded streets, and grip the steering wheel through white knuckles asking myself what in the God's name I'm doing driving alone through Mardi Gras traffic in downtown New Orleans behind an ambulance carrying my critically ill husband at ten o'clock at night. I encouraged my sisters and children to stay at my mother's house on St. Charles Avenue to watch the parades tonight, and though it didn't seem like a big deal to drive to University by myself, I'm shaking with fear and adrenaline as I circle the block several times trying to find a place to park in the dangerous neighborhood filled with inebriated Mardi Gras revelers.

At long last, I spot the hospital's parking garage on a street that intersects University Avenue and, after landing a spot on the second floor, I grab my things and sprint through the dark, deserted garage searching for the elevator, praying that I won't become the latest crime statistic in New Orleans on my way to meet Bernie. Finding the elevator in an enclosed glass hallway, I exit on the main floor where armed security guards are stationed to protect the locked hospital. The security check-point and the palpable sense of danger in the air reminds me that we're no longer in a safe, suburban neighborhood hospital, but have now entered a catch-all inner-city hospital in the most dangerous city in America. All I can do now is hope and pray that we've made the right decision in moving Bernie here.

After wandering around the deserted halls for several minutes and encountering a number of locked doors along the way, I finally find a nurse who directs me to an elevator that can take me up to the fourth-floor Surgical Intensive Care Unit where Bernie is supposed to be. Pressing the buzzer on the wall to alert the nurse's station that I'd like to come in, I announce over the speaker that I'm here to meet Dr. LeCroix and a loud buzzer and the click of a lock indicates that I may enter. Dr. LeCroix is in the hall giving instructions to the nursing staff. Looking exhausted at the end of this long day, he escorts me back to the cubicle at the dead end of the hall where he said he would put Bernie. Sure enough, Bernie is there waiting for my arrival.

"Mrs. Klein," Dr. LeCroix welcomes me with in his warm, formal manner as he shakes my hand, "I'd like to take Mr. Klein to surgery right away to perform a small procedure on his heart that will enable us to test his venous gasses. That test will tell us how much heart function he has and I'll have a better idea of where we should go from here. I need you to sign consent forms so we can conduct the procedure."

"Of course," I answer as I stand next to my husband, who is awake and listening to our conversation, though he is clearly very weak and his color has turned to ashen gray during the transfer. As the nurses reconnect his bags of medicine and try to get him situated and comfortable in this new, strange environment, Dr. LeCroix exits the room to prep for the surgery, then sends in a nurse with consent forms for me to sign. Within minutes, a team is rolling his stretcher down the hall toward surgery. Alex has arrived from my mother's house, and we sit in the waiting room nervously awaiting the results. About an hour later, Dr. LeCroix finally emerges, and his grim face tells me that the news is not good.

"Mrs. Klein," he says shaking his head as he approaches, reminding me of the gesture Dr. Madden made when he came out of the operating room on day one of this fiasco to report that he had "no idea" why Bernie was alive after the massive insult to his heart. "I'm sorry to tell you that this is much, much worse than I expected. Your husband's heart is barely beating. He is *barely* alive. His venous gasses, which measure the output of the heart, measured at thirty-three to thirty-five. Normal is sixty and when someone's venous gasses drop below fifty, they are in a severe crisis. I've never seen someone with as little heart function as your husband who has a pulse, much less who is awake, alert and communicative."

"What are you saying, Dr. LeCroix? What are you going to do?" I ask, wondering what interventions he will recommend to get Bernie's heart rate up. "Are you going to put the pressers on him again?" I inquire referring to the strong medicine they kept Bernie on continuously at Ochsner to pull his blood from the extremities and press it toward the heart.

"Mrs. Klein, that medication is only meant to be used on a short term basis because of the serious side effects it poses. Your husband's hands and feet have already turned black because he was on it for so long and, at this point, they would need to be amputated in order to get the infection in his body under control," he continues pointedly. The suggestion of amputating Bernie's hands makes my knees go weak, as his beautiful, refined hands were the first thing I noticed about him the day we met. Knowing Bernie always took great pride in his hands, I've been grateful that because he's been too weak to lift his arms, he hasn't noticed their condition thus far.

"Beside the issues with his extremities," Dr. LeCroix presses on, "Mr. Klein has a fever of 103 degrees, and I think he's far too weak to take the massive doses of antibiotics it would take to cure his infection," he continues in a beautiful French accent that cannot assuage the delivery of this terrible information. "What I'm saying is that I believe you've done everything you can do for your husband at this point. I am recommending that you disconnect all of his medication and let him go. It is futile to continue to fight to keep him alive," he continues firmly but gently.

"Will you please communicate that to my husband?" I ask as tears sting my eyes. Though I feel like I've been smacked in the face, I try to keep my composure while my daughter looks numbly at me.

"Wait, I'm so confused," Alex says to the doctor. "I thought he had an infection and we were transferring him here so you could treat that. And now you're telling us he's dying?" she questions with a note of panic in her voice that indicates she's all too familiar with the emotional trauma of this death sentence, since Bernie has received one several times during the past two months, and it's been absolutely grueling to say goodbye to him over and over again.

"Yes, I am very sorry," Dr. LeCroix offers sincerely and sadly. "I was operating under the assumption that your father had more heart function than he has. But I could not know that for sure until I had a chance to assess his heart. The test indicates that there's no way he can survive. I don't even know if he'll make it through the night, given how weak his heart is. I am really sorry," he continues gently. "Why don't you both come with me while I talk to Mr. Klein and explain what we've found," he says, as we turn to enter the locked SICU doors, and as my heart breaks at the thought of my children saying goodbye to their dad yet another time.

We walk past Marshall's room as we make our way back toward Bernie's cubicle at the end of the hall. It seems obvious to me at this point that Bernie must have sensed his imminent demise, and that's why he insisted that we "take him to University" to be where his son was. My head is spinning as we enter his room and take our positions around his bed to break the news to him, with the doctor and I flanking either side of his upper torso and Alex standing beside his legs.

"Mr. Klein," Dr. LeCroix begins as he places his hand on Bernie's right arm with mine on his left to reassure him, "the tests on your heart do not look good. Your heart is barely beating and you have almost no heart function. Frankly, I don't know how you're awake and able to communicate with us."

Bernie's wide open eyes jet back and forth between mine and LeCroix's trying to get a reading on what's coming next.

"Mr. Klein, I'm sorry to say that there's nothing else that can be done for you medically," the doctor goes on in a gentle voice that is meant to somehow balance the harsh message he is delivering. "I do not believe we can get you better, and I think the time has come for you and your wife to accept that. Therefore, I'm recommending that we disconnect the medications that are keeping you alive and let nature take its course."

Bernie looks up at me with a confused look on his face, and then speaks to Dr. LeCroix. "Are you going to euthanize me?" he asks pitifully.

"No, Mr. Klein," Dr. LeCroix assures him, "that is illegal and it is also against the laws of your Church. But there comes a point in treating a patient where we must admit there's nothing else we can do to get the patient well and we can stop treatment."

"Yes, honey," I interject solemnly, "it is considered extraordinary care when they continue to administer treatment when the burden of the treatment outweighs the benefit for the patient. A patient can choose to stop extraordinary care. But it's your decision. You're the one who has to make the decision."

"I understand," Bernie says as he looks directly into my eyes and pauses for a moment. "Judy, I've fought as hard as I can to get well. Please...I'm asking you...let me die in peace."

"Of course, I will honor your request, honey," I respond as I try to swallow the lump in my throat and fight back tears. "But we can't do it tonight. The children need one last opportunity to come to the hospital tomorrow to say goodbye to you."

"Okay," he agrees. "Doctor, you can turn everything off tomorrow. And, Judy, will you please call Fr. Beau right now to ask him to hear my last confession?"

"Yes, I'll call him right away," I respond. "Thank you, Dr. LeCroix for being willing to bring Bernie here to give us your assessment. We really appreciate your help and kindness."

"You are welcome. You can stay here with Mr. Klein through the night," Dr. LeCroix volunteers, even though I've already been informed by the nurses that the hospital is very strict about clearing the families of the patients out of the unit at night. "I'll have a recliner brought into the room so you can be more comfortable. There's also a room with bunk beds for the medical residents directly across the hall from here that you and your daughter can use to lie down. Please let me know if there's anything else I can do to make this easier on all of you," the kind doctor adds as he departs the room.

Retrieving my cell phone from my purse, I call our friend Fr. Beau to ask if he can come to the hospital immediately. "Fr. Beau," I begin, "I know it's late and the traffic is terrible, but we transferred Bernie to University for another opinion, and the doctor has recommended that we disconnect his life support. He's extremely weak and the doctor doesn't know if he'll make it through the night. Bernie has asked if you can come right now to hear his last confession."

"I'd be honored to do that. I can also administer the Anointing of the Sick to him again," he generously offers. "Listen, I can't drive because I just had surgery on my hip and I'm on crutches, so I'll have to call a friend to give me ride over there. But I'll be there as soon as I can. What floor are you on?"

"We're in the SICU on the fourth floor at University Hospital on University Avenue," I explain. "You'll have to ring the buzzer at the end of the hall so they can let you in. Call me when you arrive and I'll meet you in the hall."

"Will do," Fr. Beau says.

Thirty minutes later, my phone rings with Fr. Beau announcing his arrival. As I stand in the hallway outside Bernie's room and watch my poor friend wobble toward me on crutches, I thank God sincerely for the many holy priests who have selflessly ministered to Bernie and me these past months. This will be the thirteenth time Bernie receives the Anointing of the Sick.

After embracing Fr. Beau in the hall, I escort him into Bernie's room, then leave and close the door to give them some privacy. A short time later, Father emerges to invite me in for the anointing, whereupon he makes the sign of the cross on Bernie's forehead as he prays: "Bernie, through this holy anointing, may the Lord in his love and mercy help you with the grace of the Holy Spirit." He then anoints Bernie's wounded hands one by one and prays, "May the Lord who frees you from sin save you and raise you up." It has been incredible to watch Bernie rebound every time this sacrament has been administered, and I am ardently praying once again that God will work a miracle and heal Bernie completely.

After Fr. Beau departs, Alex and I sit beside Bernie's bed holding his hands as the nurses get him settled for the night. It's going to be another long night, and we will stay with him to watch and pray.

After Bernie falls asleep, I send a "Bernie Update" to our many friends using Alex's computer to beg for prayers.

Bernie Update: Friday, February 20, 2009

Dear Friends,

Many people are trying to call and are wondering what is happening with Bernie. After a thorough evaluation tonight by the team at University, the doctors have concluded that Bernie is septic and has almost no heart function. Because of his many complications and his weakened condition, they believe he has no chance of getting better. We have decided to remove all extraordinary support and we will surrender him to the Lord so that nature may take its course.

He is peaceful and prepared to meet the Lord. He clearly described to me in great detail the "near death" experience he had when he first arrived at Ochsner. He has great clarity on the condition of his soul and on the beauty of heaven. Fr. Beau came by tonight to hear his confession and anoint him again. All of our family will be here with him surrounding him with love and prayer. We are also asking for your continued prayers for Bernie and our family.

We are so grateful for the many graces we have received from the Lord and for the wonder of this journey. It has been filled with amazing blessings.

Much love,

Judy

February 21, 2009

Morning finally comes and Bernie has indeed hung in there through the night. The entire extended family has been alerted to come to the hospital to say goodbye to him, and our children begin to file in as soon as visiting hours begin. Kerry, Kara, Christian and Benjamin arrive, along with Bernie's two granddaughters, Kaylie and Emily and their mother Lisa. We've attained permission from the hospital to have Gaby and Grayson come in with the baby so Bernie can see his new grandson one last time, and they enter next. The mood is exceedingly somber as the children and grandchildren take turns bidding Bernie goodbye through heaving sobs, knowing we have reached the end of this long, arduous journey where we've all hoped against hope that Bernie would get well. Christian cannot even look at Bernie without falling apart completely, and Bernie indicates that he would like to have a moment to speak to him alone. As the rest of us wait in the hospital room next door that Dr. LeCroix has made available for our family to use today, Bernie spends a few minutes in private conversation with Christian, then calls each child in separately so he can give them his last guidance, advice and blessing before he departs.

Around 10:00 a.m., Dr. LeCroix comes in to instruct us about what's getting ready to happen. They will withdraw Bernie's medications one by one through the morning, spacing their removal in thirty-minute intervals while they increase the morphine in his body to counteract any pain he may experience.

I ask for a few moments to spend alone with my husband, and all I can do is sob. "I don't want you to die and I'm not ready to say goodbye!" I lament through heavy weeping. "I want you to come home with me so we can work together, honey, the way we talked about," I cry as I remember Bernie's words that we would spread the message of God's love that he has come to understand. I want to climb into bed next to him to hold him one last time, but he is still enveloped in needles and tubes that make getting physically close to him impossible. The whole scene feels completely surreal to me, like I am watching a movie of someone saying goodbye to her dying husband. Bernie, however, is at peace and he is ready to go home to God. Feeling a surge of guilt that I'm falling apart instead of giving him courage, I gather myself together and tell him not to be afraid, promising that I will be right beside him praying as he enters eternity.

"Have I ever told you how much I love you?" he asks, using one his favorite expressions that I have heard at least a thousand times by now. "All the way around the world and back again," he continues. "Never forget that."

"I love you too, honey," I respond. "Please be sure to pray for me and the children when you get to heaven. You will have to watch over us and help us."

"I will," he promises as I kiss his face one last time before the nurse comes in to administer morphine and begin removing the drips that are attached to the IV lines.

As the girls enter the room and gather around his bed, Bernie's old sense of humor breaks through the heaviness of the moment as he looks at them with a wry grin on his face and utters, "Operation Termination has now begun!" The girls scream, "Dad!!!!" in unison not knowing whether to laugh or cry, but one last joke is quite fitting from the man whose dry sense of humor made us laugh so much in life.

Within minutes, Bernie is in a deep slumber, and all of us gather around his bed crying copiously. Over the next two hours, Bernie slips into a drug-induced coma, and many members of our extended family come to say goodbye to him including Hedy and her family, his brother Henry and his wife Julie, my parents, sisters and brothers and a few close friends whom Bernie agreed in advance to allow to visit. We pray the Rosary, the Divine Mercy and the Novena to the Infant Jesus of Prague, just as we have done every day since he first got sick. We add to those the Prayers for the Dying and other spontaneous prayers for Bernie to have a happy, peace-filled death. We watch and pray as the medications come off one by one, and we stand in wait for any indication that he is beginning to slip away. Since I have become an expert at watching the monitors beside his bed that constantly mark his blood pressure and the beat of his heart, I take note as the time passes that not only are Bernie's heart rate and blood pressure not falling, they are beginning to improve. Knowing that the blood pressure medication has been sustaining his life since day one, and remembering how many times his pressure dipped to sixty over forty and the effort it took to get it back up, I'm expecting his pressure to plummet quickly now that his medication has been removed. But it does not. Oddly, his pressure is better than it has been in weeks and his heart rate has slowed from constantly racing in arrhythmia to a beat that is steady and strong.

We pray and cry throughout the day, and Dr. LeCroix comes in regularly to check on all of us. He, too, is surprised that Bernie's vital signs have improved. He informs us that this may take longer than we expected, and that Bernie may linger for a few days before his body shuts down. I prepare myself emotionally to hunker down for the duration no matter how long it takes, because come hell or high water, I am going to be beside Bernie when he dies.

Late in the afternoon, Benjamin asks if he can climb into his daddy's bed with him, now that all of Bernie's medication has been removed, and he is finally free of his IV lines and tubes. My heart aches beyond words as I watch our beautiful blond-haired "German child," as Bernie likes to call him, climb beside his dying father and put his arms around him, stating pointedly as he does: "I can still ask God for a miracle and I'm praying that Daddy doesn't die!" The confident expectation on his face and in his voice bespeak the beauty of childlike faith, and I beg God silently to have mercy and answer this precious little boy's plea. Benjamin lies peacefully next to Bernie for some time, and I marvel that he is not afraid or intimidated, especially in light of the fact that Bernie's poor body is beset by the nine weeks of unmitigated trauma it has endured.

As Benjamin exits the bed, I ask the family to leave the room for a few minutes so that I can lie next to my husband and give him one last embrace. After the nurse shuts the door and closes the curtains so we can have some privacy, I climb into the bed beside my Bernardo and do my best to wrap my arms around his limp, frail frame one last time. I remember the morning hugs we used to enjoy, when the man I slept beside for twenty-four years would put his arm out to awaken me, and I would crawl without a word to rest my head on his chest with his arms wound tightly around me. I would then fall back to sleep for a few more moments of peaceful slumber before we started the day. In the quiet of those mornings, before a word was spoken and the problems of life besieged us, all was well with the world and there was tranquility in our hearts, minds and bodies.

Those were some my favorite moments with Bernie, and I always felt deep satisfaction knowing that the intimacy of the marital bed was one of the greatest blessings and privileges of marriage. I feel none of that serenity now as I lie beside Bernie one last time; but experience only a bleak foreshadowing of the dark gulf of loneliness and grief that surely lies ahead when the person who knew me best in this world is laid to rest. "I will miss you, Bernardo," I whisper as I bathe his chest with my tears. "I love you. Please watch over us and pray for us," I plead one more time before I stand and open the door to let the children return.

Darkness descends around us and the family begins to depart one by one. Alex and Kara plan to stay with Bernie and me through the night, where Dr. LeCroix continues to provide use of the hospital room next to Bernie's as well as the bunk beds in the resident's room across the hall in case we need to lie down. One of us takes a turn sitting beside Bernie while the others lie down in the resident's bunkroom trying to catch a few winks of sleep. The night beats on with Bernie's vital signs seemingly stationed at steady and strong, though he is in a deep coma and completely unresponsive to any noise or stimulation whatsoever. Sometime in the middle of the night I decide to lie in the hospital bed in the room next to Bernie's because, after opening the curtain that separates the two rooms, I can keep an eye on him and the monitors while I lie down. The night is long and fearsome, and I lay there praying and waiting until I see the sun beginning to come up on the horizon behind the building adjacent to ours, signaling that Bernie has made it through another night.

February 22, 2009

It is 7:00 a.m. and a new nurse named Holly arrives for a shift change. The sound of the nurses conversing draws me back to Bernie's bedside so I can hear what they are saying.

"Mr. Klein has been completely unresponsive all night," the night duty nurse reports. "I bathed him and moved him around and have not been able to get any response from him whatsoever."

"Okay, I'll tell Dr. LeCroix," Holly replies as the two women turn together to walk out of the room to the nurse's desk outside the bedroom door.

Meanwhile, I am standing on Bernie's right side looking down at him when he opens his eyes wide and looks directly at me for a few seconds, then looks up at the ceiling with a startled look on his face exclaiming "Jesus!!! Do you see Jesus? Look! Jesus!!! Look!! The light!!! Do you see the light??"

"No, honey, I don't see Jesus but go to Jesus, go toward the light. It's okay, honey. You can go to Jesus," I respond reassuringly.

I begin to pray the Hail Mary softly with my heart pounding as Bernie continues to exclaim, "Judy, do you see Jesus? Look, Jesus is there! The light! The light!"

"It's okay, honey," I say again, "go to Jesus. Go toward the light."

Holly, who hears us speaking loudly, has now re-entered the room and is asking what is happening, "He sees Jesus," I tell her excitedly. "He sees the light and I'm telling him to go toward the light."

"His vital signs have not changed, Mrs. Klein, so I don't know what's going on," she says with a confused look on her face. "I'm going to give him some more morphine."

"I don't know either, but he's wide awake and he sees Jesus," I say as Kara wanders into the room half-asleep wondering what in the world is happening. For the next hour, Bernie is completely awake and insistent that he can see Jesus and the light, and no amount of morphine is effectual in stopping his celestial vision or putting him back to sleep. Kara and I begin to pray a Rosary while Bernie becomes more and more alert by the minute. Finally, he looks around the room carefully and, realizing that the son that he adores is not beside him as he's dying, says abruptly "Wait!!! Where is Christian?"

"He's not here yet, honey. It's morning and everyone except us went home to get some sleep," I reply nervously, knowing that Christian left because he flatly refuses to watch his father die.

"Well, I'm not dying until Christian gets here!" Bernie thunders in a voice that sounds so much like something Jack Nicholson would say in a blockbuster comedy; it launches us into a scene that becomes so hysterically funny that I would not have believed it possible a few moments ago. And, with Bernie's emphatic decision not to die, the dying process is stopped dead in its tracks.

"Kara," I whisper under my breath. "Go call your brother and tell him to come to the hospital immediately because Dad is awake and he's asking for him!" Kara runs out of the room in a panic to call Christian while my cell phone rings with Hedy on the line expecting a report that Bernie is close to death. "Hedy, Bernie is wide awake and has been saying for the past hour that he sees Jesus and the light!" I report.

"What????!!! How can he be awake? He was completely comatose all day yesterday!"

"I have no clue, but he's also asking for Christian and says he isn't dying until Christian gets here! Someone needs to get that kid over here right away! Bernie is asking for him!" I exclaim.

"Oh dear God! I'm on my way!" says Hedy.

"Where is Christian?" Bernie asks again. "Why isn't Christian here? The light is beginning to fade...No!! I don't want the light to fade," Bernie continues with dismay in his voice.

"Honey, Christian will be here shortly," I offer, trying to calm him down. "You just try to relax."

"Judy, there's a big problem," Bernie then tells me very seriously, switching gears completely. "The tiles on the ceiling are blocking my path and you need to take them down."

146

"What? Honey, I can't take the tiles down from the ceiling. Besides, they're not going to block your path. You're going to pass right through them," I say very reasonably.

"Judy, take the tiles down from the ceiling," he insists. "They are blocking my path and I can't leave until you take them down!" he says more insistently.

"Bernie, I can't take the hospital ceiling apart. They are not going to get in your way. Just relax and focus on Jesus," I counter, hoping to get his mind on something else.

"Judy, take the fricking tiles off the ceiling!!! Am I going to have to be in a fight with you when I die?!!" Bernie says with complete exasperation that I am not getting busy disassembling the ceiling that he is now hyper-focusing on. Suddenly, it hits me that Bernie Klein is back and he's back with a vengeance! I have always found him extremely funny, and even though he is not joking at the moment, I have the urge to go into the kind of giggling hysterics I experienced as a child when I occasionally couldn't stop laughing in church no matter how hard I tried. Sort of like the time I got the chuckles at my grandfather's funeral in the middle of the Rosary, and couldn't get a grip on myself no matter how hard my mother glared at me to stop. That same feeling is coming over me now and I spontaneously put my hands over my face in an attempt to control myself while Bernie turns to Kara, who returned from calling Christian just in time to hear the last exchange between Bernie and me, and starts in on her.

"Kara, take the tiles off of the ceiling. They are blocking my way," Bernie persists.

"Dad, I can't take the tiles off the ceiling," she says. "The hospital won't let me take the ceiling apart," she replies with gentleness and sincerity.

"Yes you can," he insists and then proceeds to banter back and forth with her as she attempts to convince him that the tiles are not an issue to his departure. "Get a piece of paper and draw a sketch of the tiles so I can tell you which ones to remove. Then call maintenance and give them the diagram so they can take those tiles down from the ceiling!"

"Okay, Dad," she says smiling, trying to suppress the laughter that is on the tip of her lips as she sees me standing on the other side of the bed with my hand over my mouth in an attempt to control my own laughter.

"Wait...are you laughing?" he asks as he looks at her with an indignant stare. "Never mind! Get Alex!" he orders. "Get out of here and get somebody in here who can get the job done!!!"

As we pour into the hall giggling like fools, Holly looks at us like we've gone completely crazy. We are downright exhausted and emotionally spent at this point and the absurdity of this scenario seems positively comical to us at the moment. Especially because it is being generated by Bernie Klein, who not only kept us in stitches for years, but who alone could be capable of creating this kind of drama around his death!

St. Thomas Aquinas taught that grace builds upon nature and Bernie's behavior right now bears witness to that great theological insight. I think we often have the misguided expectation that God will wipe out our personalities when we experience a conversion, or we think that in order to be holy, God will have to reinvent another version of us that is completely different from the original version that He created. But because our personalities are part of our unique, unrepeatable giftedness that makes us "us," God builds on who we are by nature as He redeems us. Bernie was always a stickler for details, and whether he was laboriously putting a Power Point together for a presentation or measuring within a tenth of an inch so he could hang our artwork perfectly straight on the wall, he was invested in every element of the job. It is clear that that aspect of Bernie's personality has not disappeared through all of this, because what we're seeing in the other room is classic Bernie Klein!

Kara manages to intercept Alex in the hall on her way back from the cafeteria where she has gone to get us coffee, and her face tells her sister that something is up. "What happened? Did Dad die?" Alex says with alarm in her voice as Kara walks toward her.

"No, Alex, Dad's awake and talking up a storm. He's been insisting that we take the tiles off the ceiling because they are blocking his path out of here! He's also saying that he's not going to die until Christian gets here!" Kara tells her laughing.

"Tell me you're kidding," Alex responds as her mouth falls open. "You mean we spent all day yesterday telling him goodbye for like, the fifth time, and now he's wide awake and talking again?! I mean...it's not that I want him to die, Kara, but I can't keep doing this!! I mean...live or die—pick one—but he can't keep pulling us back and forth like this! This is insanity!!!"

148

"Alex, you have to come talk to him. Mom and I have the giggles and we can't even stay in the room!" Kara continues.

Alex passes off the coffee and enters Bernie's room to find him just as Kara described.

"Alex, I need you to draw me a diagram of the ceiling and then call maintenance so they can remove the tiles that are blocking my way."

Alex tries the tactic of humoring him by telling him that maintenance is on the way, but after a few minutes, he is again insistent that she remove the tiles herself, because maintenance is taking too long to get here. Alex begins to get the giggles also, and by the time Hedy arrives, the three of us cannot keep a straight face over the stupid ceiling tiles!

"Bernie, what are you doing and why haven't you gone home yet?" Hedy asks as she enters the room and witnesses the ridiculous scene that is unfolding here.

"I keep waiting for them to come get me," Bernie says with that old boyish grin on his face, "but I don't know what the holdup is!"

He then spends the better part of the morning chatting with Hedy, and his mood has definitely lightened up because he now realizes he can lift both of his arms, which have been basically paralyzed for over nine weeks now, high into the air.

"Look what I can do!" he exclaims with energy as he takes turns lifting his arms above his head. "Judy, I don't think I'm dying anymore. The light is gone and I'm making a comeback!" Meanwhile, Christian has finally arrived and is astounded to see his father's antics.

By the afternoon, word has gotten out that Bernie Klein has experienced a resurrection and our extended family is at the hospital again to witness his resurgence. Even my cousins, who are all in town for the Bacchus parade, come to observe Bernie's revival, and he proceeds to carry on a long, entertaining conversation with four of the "M. Landrieu" sisters at once. His vital signs are still strong, though he's been off of all medications for over twenty-four hours now. And not only is he not fading, he's sharper and funnier than ever, amusing all of us with his shenanigans and lifting his arms in the air repeatedly throughout the day. We laugh until we cry all day long, and as evening closes in, Bernie is still awake and alert, and there is no sign at all that he's dying any time soon.

The family has departed again, except for Kara and Alex, and no one knows how to begin to assimilate this latest round of events, especially poor Christian. The kids' nerves are all completely shot and they are having a difficult time trying to brace themselves for what appears to be another hill in this intense emotional roller coaster ride. I have absolutely no idea what to make of this either, except to conclude that maybe God heard little Benjamin's prayer asking that his Daddy would not die.

"Judy," Bernie tells me around nine o'clock at night. "I don't think I'm dying. I want you to call the doctor and ask him to put my life support back on."

"Oh, no, no, no, no, no," I say shaking my head in response. "I do not have the nerve to ask the doctor to do that," I state, remembering Dr. LeCroix's insistent words that there was no hope that Bernie could get better, and that it's time for us to accept the fact that Bernie is dying. "If you want to ask Dr. LeCroix to put your life support back on, I'll bring him in here and you can ask him that yourself."

"Okay, bring him in here so I can tell him to reconnect my life support," Bernie says with determination.

The nurse pages Dr. LeCroix at my request and he appears within minutes outside Bernie's room. "Dr. LeCroix," I begin, "Bernie would like to speak to you. He's been awake and alert all day and it does not appear that he's ready to die."

"Mrs. Klein, I wasn't expecting him to rebound like this, but sometimes patients get a surge of energy before they die. It could take a few more days for his body to shut down," he continues "and possibly as long as a week."

"Well, my husband would like to speak to you personally," I continue as he puts on protective gear from head toe to keep himself uncontaminated from the infection Bernie is carrying.

Dr. LeCroix enters the room first, greeting Bernie in his usual formal manner. "Mr. Klein, your wife says that you would like to speak to me."

"Yes, Doctor, I wanted to tell you that I am not dying," says Bernie in a strong voice that appears to be a complete reversal of his condition when we arrived here forty-eight hours ago. "Look what I can do, Doctor," he says as he begins to lift his arms alternately in the air.

"I've had a comeback and I'd like you to reconnect my life support."

"Mr. Klein, your condition has not changed and you are still dying," the doctor informs him soberly. "It's highly unorthodox for us to disconnect a patient's life support and then reconnect it."

"I know, Doctor," Bernie says, unfazed by this assessment. "But I know that I'm not dying and I want you to reconnect my medication."

"Mrs. Klein, may I speak to you in the conference room, please?" the doctor asks me, looking completely perplexed by this turn of events.

"Sure, Doctor," I agree. "Honey, I'll be right back," I tell Bernie as I exit the room with the doctor. "Kara, please come with me. Alex, you stay here with Dad," I instruct, knowing that I am going to need Kara's help as we try to explain this to this doctor.

Outside the room, Dr. LeCroix has the night nurse page several of his associates, who are apparently still in the hospital making rounds, to come to the conference room immediately for a meeting. He then guides me behind the main nurse's station across from Marshall's room through a back hall into a dimly lit room where a large conference table sits. Two of his associates arrive within minutes, and as the five of us take seats around the table, Dr. LeCroix updates his fellow physicians on Bernie's request. I watch as the doctors shake their heads in turn indicating their disapproval of Bernie's appeal, and listen for several minutes as they discuss his case. Finally Dr. LeCroix turns to me.

"Mrs. Klein, your husband's condition has not changed. He has almost no heart function, he is septic and we do not believe there is any chance whatsoever that he can recover. He is dying, and that process can take as long as a week, sometimes even two. People don't generally ask us to turn their life support back on after it's been disconnected. Do you think Mr. Klein is mentally capable of making that kind of decision for himself?" he queries.

"Dr. LeCroix, you spoke to him. He's been awake and talking to us all day. I think he is mentally competent, but you and the other doctors will need to talk to him and make that assessment," I respond honestly.

"Okay," he replies, "we're going to go in there and explain his condition to him again. And if we think he understands what we are saying, we can let him make the decision," he says, surprising us that he's even considering what Bernie is asking as an option.

"Thank you, Doctor," I say as the five of us get up together and proceed back through the nurse's station and down the hall to Bernie's room.

The doctors all clothe themselves in protective gear in the hall before the five of us enter the room and assemble in a circle around Bernie's bed, with Dr. LeCroix standing at the left of Bernie's chest and I at the right. Dr. LeCroix launches in immediately.

"Mr. Klein, I need to let you know that you are dying. You have almost no heart function and you are septic. Your condition has not changed, even though you have experienced a surge of energy. There is no way you can survive this. That is my professional opinion, and it has been my opinion since I examined you two nights ago. I am being brutally honest with you, but I need to convey to you the severity of your condition. And I have no reason to believe that your condition will change if we reconnect your life support. Do you understand all of that?"

Bernie looks up at him with the innocence of an altar boy and says, "Yes."

"Then if you understand all of that clearly, I will let you make the decision about how you wish to proceed," the doctor concedes.

Bernie then turns to me and with absolute gravity and says "Judy, pick up my right hand," which he can no longer lift as his energy is completely expended from raising his arms all day. Having no idea what to expect next, I take his right hand in mine and elevate what is now dead weight into the air. "Make the Sign of the Cross," he instructs solemnly. Putting his hand to his forehead, I make the Sign of the Cross over his body, saying "In the name of the Father and of the Son and of the Holy Spirit" as I cross his hand over his body. Bernie closes his eyes and begins to pray interiorly. The silence in the room is deafening as the doctors stare down at him. Kara and I glance at each other nervously because the tension in the air is so thick you can cut it with a knife, while Bernie, seemingly oblivious to our presence, continues to pray for several minutes with his eyes closed as we all watch and wait. At long last, he opens his eyes and looks up at Dr. LeCroix and speaks. "I prayed about it and I want you to reconnect my life support."

"Mr. Klein," Dr. LeCroix says in a voice bordering on irritation at this late hour in the evening, which is now approaching ten p.m. and with most of these doctors having been at work since daybreak, "if I reconnect your life support, there will be no changing your mind after that. We are going to go full speed ahead with treating you no matter how hard it is or how uncomfortable you are. You will have to do everything I say without complaint, and I will not disconnect your life support again. Is that clear?" the doctor asks.

Bernie nods yes as he says, "I understand."

"And I must tell you that this is a crap shoot!" the doctor says in one last-ditch effort to spin this negatively.

"Doctor..." Bernie says with a smile on his face that only he could pull off at this moment, "I'm a gambling man. Let's do this!"

And with that nod of assent, the doctors exit the room into the hall to write orders for a reversal, which sends a team of nurses into Bernie's room within minutes to begin feverishly working to re-insert his IV lines, and get his medication up and running again. The doctor also orders immediate dialysis, as Bernie's kidneys are completely shut down and the fluid has been accumulating in his body for the past four days. Within an hour, a technician has arrived with the large, rolling dialysis machine which he attaches to Bernie methodically to begin to pull the fluid off of him. Just after midnight, the game is back on and Bernie's vital signs are stronger than ever. As he lies there wide awake with his medications in place and his dialysis running, I cannot resist asking him what he saw this morning when he kept saying that he saw Jesus.

"I saw the Infant Jesus of Prague hovering near the ceiling," he says without hesitating. "He was dressed in gold robes that were covered in rubies and diamonds and He was surrounded by brilliant light." Though Bernie conveys this information very unassumingly, it hits me like a thunderbolt. I'm not even sure if Bernie is aware of the fact that we've been praying the Novena to the Infant Jesus of Prague every day now for over two months—the one prayer card that he kept in his desk for years "in case of an emergency." Absolutely incredible!! All I can say in response is "Praise God!" as I stand in awe at how God has continually outdone Himself in manifesting His majesty and generosity as we have journeyed through this illness. I am literally astounded by what I have just heard and by the fact that, somehow, we have another chance at life. Who'd have thunk it? I almost have to pinch myself to make sure I am not dreaming.

153

After the nurse gives Bernie a good dose of sleep medication, I kiss him goodnight and head toward the resident's bunkroom. I shake my head in wonder at what has transpired here today and spend the night praising God, grinning and giggling as I replay the crazy, hysterically funny, miraculous and unexpected turn of events that visited us today. All I can feel is downright joy and excitement, and I can hardly wait to see what God is going to do next. Our God is indeed an awesome God—and the "Miracle Man" ain't too shabby either!

February 23, 2009

The day begins with Dr. LeCroix coming by first thing in the morning to tell us excitedly that he has "great news." Apparently, he and his colleagues racked their brains during the night to figure out what they can do to save Bernie, and they have come up with a plan to attach a portable, mechanical heart pump, known as an L-VAD (Left Ventricular Assist Device), to his heart to force blood to flow through the left side, which has not been pumping since the massive heart attack he sustained on December 23. Normally, these devices are used only as a short-term bridge to recovery following a heart transplant. Under that scenario, a garden hose-sized tube, which is attached to a large machine that sits beside the bed, is inserted into the heart for a couple of hours to assist a patient's heart in beating following surgery. But because the doctors want to use the L-VAD as a long-term bridge for Bernie's recovery by keeping it on him for several weeks—which has never been done before at University—they had to petition for and obtain the administration's approval to perform this procedure, which they have done successfully as of this morning. They have also secured approval from our health insurance company to pay for it.

The plan is to keep the L-VAD on Bernie for a few weeks with the aim of strengthening his heart and body by improving his circulatory function so he can recover enough to receive a smaller, extended-use L-VAD that he can go home with to prepare for a heart transplant. Needless to say, we are both elated at the news, because in spite the invasiveness and physical burden that these procedures will involve, they offer a chance at life—the one great benefit that seems to outweigh all other difficulties right now, especially after all of the close calls with death Bernie has overcome thus far.

The doctors will begin by aggressively treating the sepsis they believe Bernie is carrying with massive doses of antibiotics. Simultaneously, they will start to assemble a team of specialists for the L-VAD surgery, plus fly in the equipment and trained medical technicians to oversee the medical team as they install and set up the device. Because tomorrow is Mardi Gras Day, and there will be no getting in or out of the airport until the day after Ash Wednesday, it will take a few days to get everything and everyone in place for the surgery. We are advised to wait patiently while the operation is coordinated, and since we're not going anywhere, Bernie and I begin to settle down in this new hospital environment and we spend time telling the story of the "Miracle Man" to Holly, who will be taking care of us from now on. I also use the time to reassemble the room "decorations" that are still in my car from the previous hospital and attempt to make the glass cubicle feel homier by taping pictures, banners and cards all over the walls and doors, including 8 x 10 photos of Baby James chronicling his growth and development from December 24 until today. I then write a "Bernie Update" to our ever-growing list of family and friends to apprise them of the latest developments in Bernie's case.

Bernie Update: Monday, Feb. 23, 2009

Dear Friends:

Though we expected to be planning a funeral this week, God intervened and apparently convicted Bernie that this is not his time to die. Bernie has reversed his decision to stop life support and the doctors have begun aggressive treatment for his sepsis. The first necessary step is to find and cure the bug in his blood. Though there is only a very slim chance they will succeed, we have another opportunity to beseech the Lord for healing. If they succeed in curing his infection, they will move to step two, which is to put a mechanical heart pump in him. The doctors say this is all a "crap shoot," but Bernie has put himself in God's hands, and besides, he has informed the doctors that he is "a gambler."

You can only imagine the emotional roller coaster we have all been on, as we spent all day Friday crying, praying and saying goodbye. Yesterday, Bernie rebounded with a vengeance, and he was so funny and entertaining that we laughed until we cried all day long. I even laughed throughout the night as I thought about the funny things Bernie said during the day. Only Bernie Klein could create so much drama!

I have no idea what the ultimate outcome will be in this saga or what God has planned. I have stopped guessing at what God is doing here. I can only say that we have another chance for life and we are going for it. Please pray for the doctors to locate the source of the infection and successfully cure it.

All glory be to God.

Love,

Judy

The rest of the morning is spent reading Bernie some of the hundreds of e-mails that are being sent to us daily, including a couple from people that he helped in various ways through the years who have specifically asked that I read their letters to him out loud. A noticeable theme that has begun to develop in the notes being sent is the topic of Bernie's generosity, which many people were the lucky recipients of over time. If someone came to Bernie with a need or in a crisis, he would generally drop everything else that he was working on and put their problem on the front burner until it was resolved, oftentimes working free of charge. Though I often complained that he was creating financial trouble for us by working for others for free, he genuinely enjoyed helping people with difficult issues, and he was like a pit-bull who refused to give up when trying to solve a problem.

One recent beneficiary of his generosity was the Irish-born owner of a record company whom he met at a marketing convention where he was promoting Kara's CDs. Susan, who eventually became like a sister to him, had shared with him at the convention her heartbreak over being sued by her own sister, whose CDs she had been producing and selling for many years. Bernie offered to help her and the next thing I knew, she, her husband Ron and their two grown children were at our home for days, wherein Bernie spent countless hours with them developing a strategy to help Susan defend herself from the lawsuit and save her ailing company. Susan eventually went on to gain a judgment in court that she was very happy with, thanks to Bernie's help, and she's just called to say that she and Ron are driving down to New Orleans right now to thank him personally for all he's done for them. Meanwhile, we received an e-mail from Susan's son today expressing his gratitude for the difference Bernie's help made in their lives, which I read aloud to him:

Judy,

> *Please tell Bernie, thank you. Thank you for giving back my family our freedom. Thank you for empowering my mother and giving her the strength she needed to stand up for herself. Thank you for being the rock that she was able to lean on and turn to in these tough times. Thank you for being a friend to my mom and dad. I know they truly value that friendship.*

> *Finally, tell him I personally thank him. He was an inspiration to me and gave me a drive to be more successful both personally and spiritually.*

Sincerely,

Phil

Another recipient of Bernie's generosity was a young painter and recovering drug addict named Chris, who was part of a crew of workers that came to our home after the tree fell through the house. When Bernie learned that Chris was interested in computers and graphic design, he literally grabbed him off of the painting crew and brought him to his office to put him behind a brand new Mac computer to teach him how to design websites. That was three years ago and the two of them have designed many websites, brochures and ads since, along with producing a number of award winning videos for various projects. Chris has just written and asked that I read his letter to Bernie, which I am elated to be able to do.

Bernie,

> *When I met you in January of 2006, I was painting your house and never knew that would be the last time that I touched a paintbrush. That*

day would start a business relationship that would have such an impact on my life.

You took me under your wing and helped me become the man that I am today. Though it was only three years, I truly believe that God orchestrated such an event. I always ask God why he blessed me with such wonderful parents, a wonderful wife and having the opportunity to work with Bernie Klein. I know you think that you were hard on me sometimes, but I want you to know that I never held anything against you and learned from every circumstance that we encountered.

You became more than a boss, more than a friend—you became a father figure to me and I enjoyed and cherished every moment that we spent together. I will never forget the times that we shared together throughout the last couple of years, the time you took to explain things to me that I didn't understand, and I will never forget that you believed in me and were willing to help me get where I am today.

Bossman, one of the biggest things that I have learned from you is that generosity goes a long way. You were always willing to help someone when they needed it, you never held a grudge against anyone, and no matter what circumstance that came your way, you never lost faith because you knew that God was your provider.

Thank you for all that you've done for me and for the opportunity that you gave me. I love you and will never forget the times we spent together.

Chris

Though I boohoo as I read the letters to Bernie, he just smiles. He is full of peace and seems to be holding a deep contentment within his heart and soul that transcends natural explanation in these difficult human circumstances. Oddly, Bernie's heart rate has returned to a normal eighty beats per minute for the first time since he had the heart attack, even though they are giving him the same meds he was on at Ochsner, where his heart was always erratically racing between 130 and 170 beats a minute. Additionally, he has been fever free with no trace of an infection since he saw the Infant Jesus, though the doctor still insists he is septic and started him on a massive dose of antibiotics last night just in case. All things considered, Bernie is doing remarkably well and is feeling strong, and he's even agreed to allow a few friends to come visit, including Susan and Ron, who will be here by tomorrow morning.

Meanwhile, several of our friends are busy planning a large fundraiser for our family next weekend, where Kara will put on a "mini-concert" of her songs, including the one she wrote for the brain-damaged Florida woman named Teri Schiavo entitled "Beautiful Still." The song was featured on EWTN the night Teri died on March 31, 2005, after her husband won a long court battle to remove her nutrition and hydration against her parents' wishes. It's sure to be a very emotional night, and I'm hoping Bernie will continue to be stable enough for me to attend the event so I can thank everyone personally for their love, prayers and financial help. Though totally out of character and another positive indication of the change in him, Bernie has asked about our finances only once since he got sick, and that was not long after he told me about his near death experience. All he said was, "Judy, I have a sense of peace that our finances are being taken care of. Is that right?"

"Yes, that's right, honey. God is taking care of everything we need," I said truthfully, because though his income as a consultant pretty much came to a screeching halt on December 23, except for a monthly stipend from a dear friend and client of his named Sandy who's continued to pay Bernie out of the kindness of his heart, the contributions provided by family and friends thus far have been enough to pay all of our outstanding bills, which have mounted to around $30,000 since he got sick. I imagine that this is somewhat like what the Israelites experienced when they were wandering in the desert and God provided manna from the sky for them to eat. They never had more than they needed, but they did have all that was necessary to sustain them and allow them to keep going. There is an acute sense of God's miraculous provision for our needs from day to day, and I expect that He will continue to provide as we go forward. I'm hopeful that the fundraiser next weekend will carry us through next month's financial demands, and I gratefully await God's provision, which has come directly through the generosity of others, including the meals that are still being delivered to our home on a daily basis by friends and people from our parish church, and where Jo Jo is still holding down the fort.

By noon, Bernie is sleeping peacefully, and I take the opportunity to walk five blocks away to attend Mass at Immaculate Conception Catholic Church on Baronne Street, directly across from the newly renovated Fairmont-Roosevelt Hotel where Bernie and I spent our last wedding anniversary in July. I remember the fun we had every year "doing" New Orleans for our anniversary, when Bernie's friend and client Blaine Kern, Jr. would get us a hotel room for a weekend annually as a "trade out" for some of the work Bernie did for him. Bernie was always willing to work for cash or for a "trade out"—and he got some *great* trade outs over the years.

As I cut through the long formal corridor of the luxurious hotel to get to the church, I pass the Sazerac Restaurant where Bernie had asked my parents for permission to marry me over an elegant, formal dinner one spring night in 1985.

"I'm worried about your age and about what will happen in the future," had been my mother's first response to Bernie's query, noting that she was concerned that Bernie was fifteen years older than me.

"Me too!" Bernie offered with a poker face before smiling broadly, bringing levity to a rather awkward moment and winning my mother over immediately with his comic wit. That would be the first of many times that he brought her to laughter with his deadpan humor, which over the course of the years she has come to find as funny as I do. One particular story that my mother loves to tell is about the time in 1986 when I was pregnant for Alex and the three of us traveled together to Santa Anita Racetrack in California, where a racehorse that we owned a share in (yes, another trade out!) was running in the Breeder's Cup. After the race, which the horse performed badly in, a very important client of my mother's from her years as a Washington D.C. lobbyist for the hospital industry took us to dinner at a swanky L.A. restaurant.

Jerry, who owned several horses himself, proceeded to badger Bernie throughout the meal about what his plans were for the horse. Instead of admitting to Jerry directly that he wasn't involved in the managerial decisions concerning the horse, as we were only silent partners, Bernie repeatedly tried to put him off by answering: "I don't know." On Jerry's sixth attempt to get an answer to his question of what Bernie was planning to do with the horse, Bernie looked him straight in the eye and squarely announced, "I'm going to shoot the son-of-a-***** right between the eyes!" The poor man looked stunned, and my mother nearly fell off her chair laughing hysterically at the exchange. She had long become a fan of Bernie's sense of humor by then, and she eventually forgot that he was so much older than me. Until the heart attack.

Exiting the hotel after my trip down memory lane, I enter the church and genuflect solemnly, recalling as I do the last time I came here to pray for a sick person. It was the week Marshall died, when Bernie and I walked here several times to beg God to heal him. I never dreamed that I'd be back in this place praying the same thing for Bernie just four short years later, but I'm happy to know this oasis of prayer and peace is just blocks away from the hospital because we'll apparently be staying there for a while. Kneeling in the Church before a stunning mosaic of Our Lady of Prompt Succor, I pray the Memorare on Bernie's behalf:

"Remember O most gracious Virgin Mary, that never was it known that anyone who fled to your protection, implored your help or sought your intercession was left unaided..." Though feeling completely emotionally exhausted from all we have been through during the past week, I am still praying that Bernie can make a full "miraculous" recovery and am hoping against hope that he will. I will not allow myself to believe that God would have saved him this many times only to let him die now, and I'm convinced that Bernie and I will eventually be in ministry together, telling this story to others.

Mass begins shortly thereafter and when it concludes, I hurry back to the hospital, where Dr. LeCroix informs me that it will probably be at least a week until everything is in place for Bernie's surgery. Though a week of waiting seems like an eternity to me, it sure beats the heck out of spending this time doing what I expected to be doing, and I'll take a week of waiting for surgery over planning Bernie's funeral any day.

The rest of the week is fairly uneventful, other than arranging for visits with several friends who have asked to see Bernie face to face. Susan and Ron come on Mardi Gras Day and stay a good hour, having driven all the way down from Iowa to tell Bernie personally about the judge's positive decision regarding their lawsuit, which was issued while Bernie was unconscious, and to thank him for the difference his intervention made in their lives. Notwithstanding the fact that Bernie is flat on his back and sixty pounds lighter than the last time they saw him, you could hardly tell by their dialogue that Bernie had been near death only days ago. After listening to a detailed report on the court proceedings, Bernie launches right in to his helping mode, giving Susan specific instructions on what she needs to do next to get her business back on track. The visit ends with a conversation about plans for this year's United Catholic Music and Video Association Awards, which Susan founded in the Jubilee Year 2000, but which Bernie took the helm of last year, planning and executing the entire awards show almost single-handedly without charging a dime for his services. Held in New Orleans, the show was the largest and most elaborate the UCMVA ever had, and Bernie's vision was to make the City of New Orleans, with its deep musical roots, the permanent home of the annual ceremony which honors the best musical talent in the Catholic music industry.

"Next year's show will be the biggest ever," Bernie assures Susan as she prepares to leave. "We've got to get Catholic artists into the mainstream," he continues, echoing once again their many conversations about how to raise the stakes in getting Catholic musicians, including our daughter Kara, to be taken seriously in the Christian music world.

"You get out of here so we can get going with planning," Susan says in her soft, Irish brogue. "But for now, my friend, thank you for giving us our life back," she offers as she kisses his forehead and departs.

The other visitors who come by are two of Bernie's best friends, Sandy, who owns a trucking company, and Butch, who is a Louisiana

State Senator. Though they laugh and joke with Bernie, I can see how upset they are about his condition by the looks on their faces. Butch fights back tears as he stands over his friend's sickbed, and I leave the three of them alone for a few minutes so they can speak privately. Bernie shares with them his journey to heaven and the love of God he has come to know, and it apparently has a profound effect on Butch, who writes me the following e-mail later in the day to share his thoughts about their visit.

Dear Judy,

After Sandy and I saw Bernie today we both expressed how grateful we were to have the opportunity to talk to our friend after his heart attack. You and the kids, his family, were the most important thing in his life and there was hardly a time that we spoke when he didn't speak of you. He also talked about his mother and the tough times she had raising her children. Through all the difficulties and the times of joy, he was grateful for all of you. When we visited, we talked about the changes he would make to improve the quality of your lives. I was able to share the positive effect all of this has had on my own spirituality. He shared the Light.

Bernie and I both felt the ability to tell each other about things we wouldn't ordinarily share. I think it was just a confidence that we recognized early on that we were nothing special, just a couple of guys struggling along trying to be the best people we could be. There were a lot of times when we met for business, but talked about everything else in the world, and then gave ten percent of the meeting for the purpose of the meeting. While traveling from a meeting in Lafayette back to Baton Rouge a couple of years ago he asked me if I thought he was a good person. When I paused to develop my answer, he laughed and said that the pause was answer enough. I can't remember what I said in response but he knew that I respected him and that I wouldn't have spent that much time with a person I didn't value.

With love,

Butch

I am deeply touched by the sentiments Butch shared and by the insight that although Bernie always claimed he was a "good person," he was still actively seeking that affirmation from people in his life before he got sick. It occurs to me that Bernie's sometimes-outrageous behavior was probably driven by that need for affirmation, especially since he never got that gift from his own father.

As the sun begins to set and Bernie finds sleep, I hear the Mardi Gras crowd outside winding down the celebration and make my way to the window to watch the throngs of revelers leaving the biggest party on earth. "Laissez the bon temps roule," I think as I watch the festivities below from a distance. "Yes, Lord," I pray, "please do let the good times roll."

March 4, 2009

A team of nurses comes to get Bernie at 8:00 a.m. to wheel him into surgery, where he will receive a Centri-Mag Blood Pump. Dr. LeCroix has informed me that the operation will take several hours and that there's a fifty-fifty chance that Bernie won't make it through, given his weak and compromised condition. Kara, Alex, Christian and I are instructed to wait in the Surgery Waiting Room, where the doctor will come out to give us a report as soon as he is done. The sense in my spirit is that Bernie is going to come through the surgery just fine, and around eleven a.m., Dr. LeCroix enters the waiting room to inform us that Bernie made it through with flying colors.

"It went much better than I expected," the doctor conveys with relief. "I'm hoping that we're going to see an immediate improvement in his overall condition, but it should be very obvious right away whether this is going to work," he continues. "He's either going to sink or swim, Mrs. Klein. Let's pray that he swims."

"Thank you so much for being willing to try this, Dr. LeCroix," I respond with sincere gratitude. "I'm going to continue to do what I know how to do, and that's pray."

"Yes, please do," he continues. "You can go back to his room now to wait for him there. The nurses will wheel him in as soon as he's out of Recovery."

Within an hour, I spot a team of nurses wheeling Bernie's stretcher down the hall, pulling beside them a machine that is the size of an ice chest that sits atop a stainless steel table with wheels. I am surprised by the sight of the blood pump; not only because it is larger than I expected, but because it has two transparent garden size hoses running in and out of it, allowing an unnervingly clear view of Bernie's blood as it is circulated through his body. His chest is completely bare to allow medical access where the tube enters his body, giving me a view of Bernie's side that takes my breath away. The first thing I notice is that the doctor has made a two-inch incision through his right rib, sending a chill down my spine as I note its likeness to the wound in the side of Christ.

"He's received the fifth wound of Jesus," I say to Alex with my mouth agape as we stand beside Bernie's bed observing the remarkable likeness of the wounds in Bernie's hands, feet and side to the five sacred wounds of Christ received during His Crucifixion—the devotion to which was made popular in the Twelfth Century by Bernie's namesake, St. Bernard of Clairvaux, who also wrote the Memorare. St. Paul tells us in Galatians 2:20: "I have been crucified with Christ; and it is no longer I who live, but Christ lives in me." The marks on Bernie's body, called the "stigmata" in the Greek translation of the Bible, bear visible witness to the suffering Christ, who has inhabited Bernie's personal agony with His presence in a manner that is quite profound and unmistakable.

Several hours later, Bernie wakes up and is in quite a lot of pain from the surgery. Though he has gotten some relief in the past, especially from the bedsore on his back, by being rolled from side to side by the nurses, he must remain fairly stationary now to avoid pulling the L-VAD tubes out of place. In light of the fact that he still has a large, extremely painful wound on his back, it becomes quickly evident that he will need larger doses of pain medication to keep him comfortable. I can see that he is using all of his energy to stay calm and focused, as the machine attached to his body is not only noisy and overwhelming, but takes up most of the space on the right side of the room, leaving very little space for anyone to sit comfortably beside him as the medical staff comes in and out to check his status. Nevertheless, we both promised Dr. LeCroix when he agreed to reverse the life support decision, that we would push forward without complaining even in the face of severe discomfort, and it seems that Bernie and I are both going to be given the opportunity to put our money where our mouth is.

The thrilling surprise is that Bernie's kidneys begin to work almost immediately now that his blood is circulating throughout his body, and we are all ecstatic at seeing a bag of urine begin to fill up, indicating that he may not need permanent kidney dialysis after all. I would never have expected the sight of urine to bring such a strong positive reaction, but it's amazing what several months in the ICU can do to change one's priority list concerning what's important.

Dr. LeCroix sends in a physical therapist to begin moving Bernie's arms and legs, wanting to take advantage of the window of opportunity available to get him stronger. He also encourages me to move Bernie's arms and legs hourly, which I agree to do despite my intimidation over the machine that's now an appendage on my husband's body. Due to the support his heart is getting in beating, Bernie's vital signs are the strongest they've been since Christmas, and our nurse Holly assures me that his condition is now very stable, in spite of how things look. She also starts giving him ice chips to give him practice swallowing in preparation for beginning to eat solid food, which Dr. LeCroix hopes to introduce in the near future if he continues to make headway.

Bernie makes nice progress for the rest of the week and is in pretty good spirits due to the fact that things seem to be going well from a medical standpoint, as long as they continue to manage his pain. When Saturday rolls around, I decide to attend the benefit for our family, which is being held at the gorgeous, plantation-style home of Jane and Bobby Harvey, a devout and big-hearted couple known for their magnanimity in volunteering their homestead for fundraisers. Strange as it feels, I exchange the standard sweat suit I've been wearing in the hospital to keep me warm for a pretty party dress, and I head out with all of the children to the event being held on our behalf. As expected, Kara's songs garner buckets of tears from everyone in attendance. I have to say it's the first time I've ever been to a lavish party where the guests all sobbed before dinner.

Returning home around eleven p.m., I call the hospital to check on Bernie before falling into my bed for the night, which feels like a grand luxury right now. Having slept on chairs, floors, bunk beds, hospital beds and sofas these past months, I can hardly remember the last time I slept at home in my very own bed. I sleep soundly and peacefully, enveloped in the love of many friends and a number of strangers who came together out of sheer kindness to incarnate charity for us. Well rested on Sunday morning, I snuggle with Baby James and enjoy a homemade double cappuccino before sending out a Bernie Update and heading back to the hospital.

Bernie Update: Sunday, March 9, 2009

Dear Friends:

The doctors are very pleased with Bernie's progress since he received the heart pump on Wednesday. His kidneys began to work immediately, praise God, and they have improved steadily all week. The doctors hope to remove his dialysis catheter this week, as well as his trach tube. Plans for this week also include hourly workouts throughout the day to rebuild his body and getting him to eat real food. Bernie is in good spirits and has been exceptional about pushing past the pain and discomfort he is feeling in order to rebuild his muscles. He is determined to get well, and has not complained once about how much he has been through or the constant moving, poking and prodding that is part and parcel with being in the ICU.

As far as the long term plan goes, there are three possibilities. One is that this pump will stimulate his heart to begin beating at a life sustaining level. (Yes, this is a very long shot and it will take another miracle, but why not ask the Lord for another one?) The second option is to put in the Heart Mate II, which requires open-heart surgery to attach a mechanical pump to Bernie's heart, but would give him the opportunity to go home and wait for a heart transplant. The third option is to go directly from this pump to a heart transplant, but he would have to get strong enough to survive heart transplant surgery and all that goes along with that intervention. For now the focus is getting him stronger and getting him out of ICU to a regular room.

On a personal note, thank you from the bottom of my heart to Jane and Bobby Harvey, Cecil and Johnny Beatrous, Angele and Gary Darling, Suzy and Steve Neal, Celie and Dan Clark, and Ann and Tony Costa for hosting such an incredible benefit for our family last night. Thank you also to all of those who attended or contributed to the event. I have truly never felt so loved and honored and am so very grateful for the support and generosity so many people have demonstrated to us during this crisis. Words simply do not do justice to what is in my heart...I can only say thank you, thank you, thank you.

With love and blessings,

Judy

March 12, 2009

Although we've been riding high since the surgery, Bernie takes a sudden turn for the worse. He has developed an infection in his lungs, causing his temperature to spike, and he's becoming visibly weaker as his breathing begins to be labored. Most alarming is the fact that his body is not absorbing nutrition through his feeding tube, causing the space outside the blood vessels, called "the third space," to swell rapidly. This morning, while moving his arms in circles for exercise, I noticed that one of his arms was much larger than the other, and I could feel blood clots in his swollen upper arm. Feeling a wave of panic at this obviously abnormal development, I call Dr. LeCroix immediately, who confirms that Bernie is now moving rapidly in the wrong direction. In his opinion, the only thing left to do is to cease tube feeding, and begin mouth feeding immediately in the hopes this will reverse the trend and kick start his body in assimilating nutrition. But before that happens, a swallow test must be conducted to ascertain whether Bernie can take food by mouth without aspirating.

After sending a very brief but urgent e-mail requesting prayer, I sit alongside Bernie while the respiratory therapist mixes blue dye into a cup of vanilla pudding then spoon feeds him a couple of bites. Watching anxiously as she suctions his tracheostomy, it is impossible to miss the blue dye that appears in the suction tube indicating that food is indeed entering his airways. I'm all too aware that this is Bernie's last hurrah, and the room is heavy with disappointment as it becomes obvious that consuming food orally is not an option. Dr. LeCroix enters the room shortly thereafter, and asks if he can speak to me alone. After we exit into the hall and close Bernie's door, he drops the bomb.

"Mrs. Klein, it's hopeless. The intervention with the mechanical heart pump has failed and there's nothing else we can do. We will continue with the heart pump and all of his medications, but I expect Mr. Klein to experience respiratory failure in the next few days as his body and lungs fill with fluid."

His words fall like a hammer to my heart, and I burst into tears and begin sobbing. "I'm sorry, Mrs. Klein," the doctor continues solemnly.

"We knew this was a crap shoot from the start. I wish there was more we could do, but I hope that your conscience is clear that we've tried everything possible. I'll come in with you to explain the situation to Mr. Klein."

"Thank you doctor, but I'd like to tell him myself," I say as I shake his hand, and as Holly, who has become our new defender, glares at him from behind as he walks away. She then puts her arms around me for a big hug saying, "That was too rough!"

"I need a few minutes to compose myself before I go back in," I tell Holly before running into the bathroom inside the resident's room to cry. "Please tell my husband I'll be right back." After about twenty minutes of weeping and wrestling with God about why He would allow our hopes to be resurrected only to have them dashed again, I splash cold water onto my eyes, put on my bravest face, and re-enter Bernie's room to break the news to him. But before a word leaves my lips, he says, "You've been crying...I'm dying, aren't I?"

I've never had a poker face—though I've certainly wished for one during the past months—because whatever I'm carrying on my face generally speaks volumes to Bernie about how he's doing. "Yes, honey, you are," I say gently as I pull up a chair beside him and wrap my hands around his arm.

Looking up at me with the expression of a terrified child, Bernie utters, "I'm scared!" This is the only time that he has mentioned fear since day one of this ordeal, and the look in his eyes breaks my heart. "It's okay, honey," I offer with firm reassurance. "You are not going to do this alone. I promise that I'll be beside you praying as you enter heaven. I am not going to leave your side."

"Judy," he then says more reflectively. "I've fought as hard as I can fight. I'm done. I'm ready to go in peace." There is a certainty and resignation in his voice that gives me a sense of clarity that I have not experienced until this present moment that the battle for Bernie's natural life is, in fact, at its conclusion.

I call the children to tell them the news and let them know that they have another opportunity—again—to say goodbye to Bernie, who is now sleeping the majority of the time. Gaby and Christian are coming now and Kerry will arrive this evening. Kara will come tomorrow on her way to a healing retreat in Natchez with Fr. Jerry Drinkwater—the same exorcist who led the healing retreat that Gaby and I attended in November—but which she's now wondering if she should cancel. I assure her she should attend the retreat, because Dr. LeCroix has indicated that we could be here for another week waiting for the dying process to take place. She has said her goodbyes repeatedly to her father, and unless she feels the need to stay, she's free to go and spend some time beginning to heal from all of this. Alex is on her way and will stay with Bernie and me until he has departed this life. She wants to be with her dad when he dies, so we will wait this out together.

At some point in the afternoon, it becomes obvious that Bernie is very uncomfortable and I call the nurse to administer more medication. "How are you handling all of the pain?" I ask, amazed that he has not complained once about his suffering since the day he had the apparition of the Infant Jesus of Prague.

"When I think I can't take it anymore, I close my eyes and see Jesus on the Cross, and I see Mary at the foot of the Cross helping. I think 'if He could do that for me, I can do this,'" Bernie responds with no tinge of resentment or resistance in his voice, only acquiescent acceptance as he readies himself to meet the Lord. And as Bernie bears his suffering silently and embraces his imminent end, I feel a sea change in my own acceptance level concerning his death, because for the first time since December 23, I'm at peace that it's okay to let go and say goodbye.

Before now, everything within me rose up to fight like hell for Bernie's life. I was not about to take "no" as an answer from God when I prayed that He would heal my husband's heart, and I was still grasping for "my will" to be done. But seeing the peace in Bernie's face as he rests in the presence of God gives me the firm assurance that my prayers have indeed been answered—those many years of prayers that Bernie would come to know and trust God as his loving, merciful Father. I understand now that Bernie has received just the healing he needed in the specific and personal way he needed it, as have I. Because what I was praying for all along for Bernie is precisely the miracle that I needed for myself, and this journey has brought me to that resting place at long last. I can see clearly now that God has never been out to get Bernie or me, and that He has been ever so carefully working all of our sufferings together for our good, for our sanctification, for our redemption. As I experience God's sweet presence and splendor resting right here with us, I know with certitude that it is finally time for Bernie and me to both go home.

Holly, who has been taking care of us now for over two weeks, notices the change in me, though I was unaware how obvious it was that I was still holding on with all my might when we disconnected Bernie's life support just two short weeks ago.

"I can see that you are finally prepared to say goodbye," our precious nurse says, as I walk past her desk toward the bathroom. "You were nowhere near ready when you first got here," she continues with the honesty and boldness of a nurse who sees people die on practically a daily basis. "But you're ready now."

That unsolicited feedback gives me a peculiar sense of confidence that I can do this, and that Bernie and I are both going to be okay. The drama in the air has finally dissipated, and there is no more denial, wheeling or dealing. There will be no grandiose goodbyes this time and no more encore appearances—only serene surrender to Our Father in heaven, who awaits Bernie's arrival.

March 13, 2009

I begin the day by writing a "Bernie Update" to tell our family and friends about the latest developments here.

Bernie Update: Friday, March 13, 2009

Dear Friends,

Sadly, the news from the doctors is not good. They have been unable to reverse Bernie's inability to assimilate nutrition and his liver is failing. He has also developed an infection in his lungs and his breathing has become labored. The doctor is going to continue to treat him with antibiotics, but expects him to experience respiratory failure in the next few days. The heart pump, food and fluids will continue, but the focus will become comfort as we wait and pray.

This is obviously not what we were hoping for, but we knew going into this intervention that the chances of success were slim. I am grateful that we tried and am so proud of Bernie for his courage, strength and humility during this long ordeal. He has fought with every ounce of his being, and has never complained about how much suffering he has endured. We have been graced with prayer, love and many blessed conversations, and our entire family has been able to communicate to him how much we love and appreciate him.

I am at peace that we tried everything and have surrendered Bernie again to the Lord. If the Lord wants to work a miracle and heal him, of course that is His privilege and I would be delighted. But I know that the ultimate healing is to see God face to face in heaven and that is the destiny we hope for and wait for.

Thank you for your ongoing prayers for grace, healing and peace. The Lord has demonstrated His kindness and mercy to us repeatedly through these months, especially through the many people he has sent to love and support us through this trial.

175

Blessings and love,

Judy

Hedy calls not long after to say that Fr. Jerry will be landing soon and that Kara will arrive at the hospital with him as soon as she picks him up at the airport. Knowing what a gifted priest and healer this man is, I'm excited that he's agreed to come, if for no other reason than to give Bernie a final blessing and administer the Sacrament of the Sick once more before he dies. If the Lord wants to surprise us and restore Bernie's health, indeed I would be thrilled. But I have finally let go of that outcome and accepted that Bernie's dying isn't "bad" news; in reality, it's grace. Having embraced that deeper truth, I am focused now only in assisting Bernie on his journey to eternal life.

The day is quiet and still, and all of the activity that has been whirling around us is finally winding down. We pray all of our regular prayers once more, and Alex sits with Bernie as I walk to noon Mass. I feel an other worldly sense of peace as I kneel in adoration during Mass, knowing that soon Bernie will be among the heavenly host that worships God in eternity—watching, waiting and praying for me as I continue my earthly journey.

Late in the afternoon, Kara calls to say that she and Fr. Jerry have arrived at the hospital, and I walk down to the waiting room to greet the old priest and apprise him of the situation. Sharing with him only the medical details of Bernie's case and the doctor's assessment that Bernie's body has begun the dying process, I tell him nothing about the vision Bernie had of his own wounded heart, with one side beautiful gold and the other side blue, looking like "ugly debris." Nor do I share anything about Bernie's near death experience, where he was told by God to go back and make amends for his life.

"Okay," Fr. Jerry says very matter-of-factly when I conclude with the medical report. "Well, let's go ask the Lord to heal him." The three of us enter the SICU and together and make our way down the long hallway to the end room, where Bernie and Alex are waiting. Fr. Jerry enters and greets Bernie, then anoints Bernie's forehead and hands with oil, saying the prayers for the Anointing of the Sick over him for the fourteenth time. He then puts his right hand on the top of Bernie's head, and after praying momentarily in silence, smiles widely as he begins to speak.

"Ahhh," Fr. Jerry exclaims slowly as he continues to smile, obviously moved with deep satisfaction and approval over what he has heard from God. "This man has a heart of *pure* gold," Father adds as Kara, Alex and I begin to weep, remembering full well the clear vision Bernie had of his divided heart and the purification he said he needed. "Bernie," Fr. Jerry continues as Bernie looks up at him with wide eyes, "God the Father wants you to know that your generosity is a direct reflection of *His* generosity in heaven and that He is so pleased with you. So pleased! Well done, Bernie," Fr. Jerry declares, smiling wider all the while. "Well done!"

It's hard to miss the echo of God the Father's thundering voice at Jesus' Transfiguration in Matthew 17:5, where Christ is transformed into a vision of heavenly glory before his apostles' eyes at the culmination of His public life. "This is my beloved Son in whom I am well pleased!" the Father's voice affirmed. It suddenly dawns on me that *this* is what Bernie Klein has been waiting for to die; and that this is precisely the gift that Our Heavenly Father wanted to give him so he can finally rest in peace. In the absence of his own father's blessing, Bernie spent years seeking affirmation from others—including and especially me—often engaging in over-the-top behaviors that spawned trouble for him in an attempt to grasp at human approval. Now that all is said and done, it strikes me that he's finally received the one blessing that could possibly satisfy his longing—and the only endorsement that truly matters in the nod of God the Father.

It is apparent that the Father has been preparing Bernie to receive His heavenly glory, transforming him before our very eyes into a temple fit to hold it. I can perceive the dance that's taken place between God's glory and both of our brokenness throughout these hallowed months, as Our Father pushed back our wills and walls to make room for His increase in us. It took a lot for us to lift our puny gates and let Him enter in—moving our own constructs from front and center stage so more of His love could inhabit our small temples. It was indeed the force of suffering that pried our portals open, letting in the fresh new air of penetrating love as we surrendered to its transforming power. *That's* what's been happening to Bernie and to me during this long and painful exodus, one that took us out of the terrain of own stone-set expectations and jarring disappointments to this unforeseen yet promised land of trusting surrender in God's holy presence.

Without much fanfare, Fr. Jerry turns and leaves the room with the girls and I am left alone with my husband, who is beginning to fade fast. "Bernie, did you hear what Fr. Jerry said to you?" I ask as he stares up at me.

"Every word," Bernie says with a quiet sense of satisfaction before adding one last thought.

"Judy, I have loved you since the day I met you and you have always been a jewel in my heart," he says, looking me directly in the eyes a final time. "Do what you need to do to take care of yourself. Get married! Take care of yourself." And with that benediction, Bernie closes his eyes in peace, never to regain consciousness again.

I pull my chair close beside him so I can keep my hands on his body as he prepares to depart, not so much to hold on to him as to give him solace, and offer him to God in the last moments of his life. I sit alongside my Bernardo reflecting on this ending, thinking about the paradox of death and the irony that this apparent defeat is the pre-requisite for eternal victory, bringing with it the opportunity to move with ease from one state of disguised splendor to the next. St. Paul captures this mystery perfectly:

"But we hold this treasure in earthen vessels, that the surpassing power may be of God and not from us. We are afflicted in every way but not constrained, perplexed, but not driven to despair, persecuted but not abandoned, struck down but not destroyed, always carrying about in the body the dying of Jesus, so that the life of Jesus also may be manifested in our body...Therefore we are not discouraged rather, although our outer self is wasting away, our inner self is being renewed day by day. For this momentary light affliction is producing for us an eternal weight of glory

beyond all comparison, as we look not to what is seen, but to what is unseen, for what is seen is transitory, but what is unseen is eternal" [2 Cor. 4:7-16].

I consider the weight of glory that has come to rest upon us during these eighty-seven winter days, leading us beyond the limits of our own deficiencies and poverties, and bringing with it an immense gravity that forced our self-enclosures wide open, letting love's new life come in. The things that Bernie and I thought were so important—like winning arguments and negotiating over who was right—have suddenly dissipated like so much dust; making way for the one thing that lasts—and that is love alone.

Alex joins me within minutes sitting beside Bernie, and Kerry comes by shortly thereafter and stays for several hours before saying one last goodbye as the day comes to a close. The mood here is markedly different than the last time we did this, and in place of the spectacle of Bernie's previous go round at dying, there is only a hushed sense of resignation in the air. A few of the nurses who cared for us these past weeks, along with several others who have not, come in throughout the evening to comfort us, and each one of them breaks down with emotion as they tell us they've heard the story of the Miracle Man and have been praying for Bernie and for our family.

"They are so breaking protocol!" Alex finally says to me after the fourth nurse comes in and begins to cry. "Are they supposed to be crying like this?" she asks with surprise. "And talking about Jesus so openly?"

"They're human Alex," I respond with an amused laugh at her incredulity over the outbursts of the nurses. "You get attached to people when you spend a lot of time with them in a hospital, and it would be impossible to do this job without faith," I say, grateful for the body of believers who have accompanied and comforted us during these three long months.

The night is dark and daunting, and though Alex and I had planned to alternate turns sleeping in the bunkroom, there is a palpable sense of death in the air that keeps us huddled close to Bernie and to each other. We offer many Rosaries as Bernie's breathing becomes more and more shallow, and as dawn finally breaks and he takes his last breath, we are holding his hands praying the Rosary for him, just as we promised. Around 6:20 a.m., the nurse comes in with a stethoscope to listen to his heart and looking at us sadly, gently says, "He's gone. I've called the doctor to come and issue a death certificate. You can stay as long as you like with him."

Numb and completely spent, but with a sense of strange satisfaction that our prayers have been very tenderly answered, Alex and I embrace and weep for a time. We then begin the process of calling the family to let them know that Bernie has gone home. Kara answers her cell phone with the words, "Dad died, didn't he, Mom? I just had a strong sense of his presence and felt him come to me to say goodbye."

"Yes, he died a few minutes ago," I verify. "We're waiting for the doctor to come now to confirm his death."

The doctor comes and goes, and though part of me wants to stay with Bernie, there is no sense of his presence here any longer. The funeral home has been called and they will be here shortly to retrieve Bernie's body. My place is now with my children, and I need to go home to them. Alex and I begin to disassemble the room and pack our things to transport them to the car. The scene feels unreal as we begin the long trek down the hall for the last time, pushing a cart full of stuff in front of us as we walk like zombies toward the nurses' station. I have just uttered the words, "Please tell Holly I said thank you for everything," to the nurse behind the desk when I spot Holly coming around the corner walking directly toward me with her arms extended. "I'm so sorry, Mrs. Klein," she says through tears as she gives me a long embrace. "I was so hopeful that Mr. Klein would make it," she continues lovingly.

"I know," I respond. "Thank you very much for everything, Holly. You have taken such wonderful care of us."

We bid the staff adieu, then exit the hospital and pack the car to make the drive home across the longest bridge in the world. It is a cold, dreary day and we are now in the throes of fresh, raw grief.

BERNIE UPDATE: SUNDAY, MARCH 15, 2009

BERNARD JOSEPH KLEIN MAY 25, 1945 - MARCH 15, 2009

Dear Friends:

Bernard Joseph Klein went to his eternal rest at 6:20 this morning. I was grateful to be beside him when he died, and he was peaceful and ready to meet the Lord.

The funeral will be held at Our Lady of the Lake Catholic Church in Mandeville on Thursday, March 19, the Feast of St. Joseph. I will update you as arrangements and times are finalized.

Thank you so very much for your love and prayers. I will always be grateful.

Blessings and love,

Judy

March 16, 2009

It's 5:00 a.m., the morning after Bernie's death, and I awaken to a dream about him. I can't remember specifically what I'm dreaming, but the moment I consciously think Bernie's name, I encounter something I've never experienced before in my life. It feels like the veil of heaven is torn open for an instant, spilling what I can only describe as "gold dust" all over me, which falls very slowly in a shimmering sensation from the top of my head to the tips of my toes as I shiver from head to foot. It's a totally different sensation than the anointing that I've experienced many times over the years when the Holy Spirit shows up during prayer, and it's clear as a bell to me that this mystical phenomenon is a tiny taste of paradise, to which I exclaim out loud in jubilation, "Bernie, you're in heaven!!!"

As soon as those words exit my mouth, I'm filled with an exquisite sense of ecstasy that leaves me feeling that I may burst with joy, and I praise God for the confirmation that Bernie is now experiencing the beatific vision in the ineffable presence of God. Though I am no mystic, saints like Theresa of Avila have described mystical experiences of God's presence, which include an experiential knowledge of God that is accompanied by spiritual joy, for which there is no natural counterpart in human experience. I figure that this must be an inkling of the ecstatic joy of heaven, and that the Miracle Man was granted permission by God to give me one last kiss, enabling me to catch a miniscule glimpse of his happiness in heaven in so doing. Not at all what I was expecting the morning after my husband's death, but I'm delighted by the unexpected gift.

Buoyed by this divine consolation, I arise to begin the process of planning Bernie's funeral, only to discover that the electricity has gone out completely in half of the house. Shaking my head over how our home continues to serve as a metaphor for our lives, I call an electrician to come fix the problem immediately, while Jo Jo, the children, and I sit at the breakfast room table and begin to pour through family photo albums to find just the right pictures of Bernie to memorialize our lives with him.

The funeral will be held on March 19, three days from now; a fitting day for Bernie's life to come full circle—marking the day his own father died and the feast day of his namesake, St. Joseph. The funeral Mass will be celebrated at our parish of Our Lady of the Lake, a 160-year-old church founded by the Benedictine monks that holds many of the deep, spiritual memories of our family, including our three daughters' First Holy Communions, Marshall's funeral and the baptism of Baby James. Kara will sing "Beautiful Dreamer," the song Bernie always said he wanted sung at his funeral, even though he told us in the hospital that he wasn't sure anymore if it was "appropriate." He will then be interred at St. Joseph Abbey, a breathtakingly beautiful stretch of land thirty minutes north of our home that houses a Benedictine monastery along with the final resting place of many of the priests and monks of the greater New Orleans area. Thankfully, the monks recently opened an additional parcel of land to be used as gravesites for the general public, enabling me to acquire two plots side by side right in front of the statue of the Blessed Mother and directly across the path from where Marshall is buried.

We take turns reading aloud the many e-mails being sent by family, friends and well-wishers who have followed our story over the Internet. One note that grabs my attention is from a physician and heart transplant recipient in Chicago whom I've never met, but who got on the "Bernie Update" list after hearing about Bernie's story.

Judy,

I prayed so hard for Bernie. It brought me to sobbing when I heard the news today. I feel I knew Bernie as I walked in his path myself. I will continue to pray for the repose of his soul. I am sure he was ready and in a state of grace. I will continue to pray for you and those that will grieve over his loss.

Peace of Christ be with you,

Dr. Ted

I am amazed by the kindness of complete strangers, who have obviously become deeply emotionally invested in our story as they've journeyed with us through this illness, and as they now weep with us over Bernie's death. Another letter arrives from Susan, sharing her thoughts about her last visit with Bernie.

Dearest Judy,

The day has finally come for Bernie to make his last trip - he ran the race—he won the prize.

Although we can not possibly feel the loss that you and the children are feeling, we just want you to know that having Bernie and all of you in our life was the greatest gift at one of the darkest times, and we will never forget his kindness and unselfish giving as he tried to solve the problems of so many people.

I smile when I think of him. When we saw him two weeks ago he was still so mentally strong and so bright and funny—even though his body struggled for life, he was still very much in control, putting everything in order and giving strength and courage and directions not only to us but I am sure to many others.

There will be a big void in our lives without him but we know as you do, he is finally at peace and happy in the arms of the Lord and in the loving care of His Blessed Mother.

Please let us know when you are planning the funeral. Ron, Susie, Phillip and I would love to come to say our last farewell to our friend.

God bless,

Susan

Between reading e-mails and planning the funeral, I sit in the warm sun on the courtyard sofa, remembering how I found refuge in this little slice of heaven on earth just three months ago when this affair of the heart began to unfold. And, though I shed copious tears as we tell stories about Bernie, I can honestly say that the predominant feeling I experience is one of deep satisfaction and joy that I was privileged to be part of his glory story—the exodus into a life-altering illness that tore our hearts apart and broke open our capacities to behold the glory of God hovering in our midst, while teaching us both to trust and to love.

The noise of Benjamin and the neighborhood children permeates the atmosphere as I breathe in the smells of the coming spring and hold Baby James snugly in my arms. Though the flowers in our gardens and ceramic pots are brown and lifeless from several hard freezes during the winter months, the azaleas are beginning to bloom and the fragrant aroma of sweet olive hangs heavy in the air, reminding me of the mysteries of death and new life that are constantly being incarnated in the world around us, bringing with them both bitterness and sweetness, agony and elation, birth pangs and deliverance.

The Miracle Man's journey taught us to stand firm in the tension of those connected realities, and that is where God showed up: outside of the little boxes of our own limited understanding and far beyond our projections of how we thought things ought to be. Instead, smack dab in the middle of the heart, with all of its tortures and triumphs, is the place where the Miracle Man learned the lessons of love—and it's where he taught them to me.

Sunday, March 22, 2009: Final Update

Dear Friends:

Bernard Joseph Klein was buried on the Feast of St. Joseph on Thursday, March 19, 2009. When we awoke, a dense fog covered the area, but by the time we arrived at Our Lady of the Lake Church, the sun had broken through, ushering in a glorious sunny day. It is difficult to share what is in my heart, but I would like to give you a glimpse of the day in Bernie's honor.

The funeral liturgy was absolutely beautiful, as we were graced with the angelic voices of Kitty Cleveland and the St. Scholastica Academy Choir under the direction of a most gifted pianist and friend, Sharon Scharmer. Fr. John Talamo, Fr. Beau Charbonnet and Fr. Robert Cavalier honored us by presiding over the liturgy, and their presence on the altar in gold robes made present to us Christ's priestly presence in heaven—sacred, redemptive, all-powerful. I have never been so happy to be Catholic as I was on Thursday. I stood in awe and wonder as I watched the rich symbolism of the funeral Mass unfold, reminding us of Bernie's baptismal vows, his presence at the heavenly banquet of the Lamb of God, his marriage to the Eternal Bridegroom. As sad a day as it was, it was equally joy filled thanks to the consolation of the hope of heaven, and the love of our family and friends—all tangible and very real to me as I stood in the church with the symbols of heaven before my eyes surrounded by people who love me, Bernie and our family.

When the funeral Mass ended, we processed to the cemetery of St. Joseph Abbey, where many of the monks and priests of our archdiocese are laid to rest. It is holy ground, full of silence, prayer and majestic oaks. As we drove up to Bernie's gravesite following the hearse, seven Marines stood at full attention waiting for his arrival. It took my breath away to see them standing there and to remember how proud Bernie was of serving in the Marine Corps—the place where he found his personal gifts and his identity as a man. A twenty-one-gun salute and "Taps" followed our prayers, along with the folding of the American flag accompanied by Kitty's gorgeous voice singing "Amazing Grace." It was a moment none of us will soon forget.

After the services concluded, we made our way to the home of our dear friends, Angele and Gary Darling. Gary is an incredible chef and he laid out a delicious banquet for us, including his famous Jamaican Jerk Chicken Salad and Mediterranean Hummus. We ate, laughed and cried as we remembered Bernie and his unique personality. A gentle wind blew through the French doors that were open throughout the house, and the Holy Spirit was very present as we shared a meal and fellowship in remembrance of Bernie. I returned home that evening with my heart full, feeling as though I had been to a wedding reception instead of a funeral. It was a happy ending to a day I had dreaded and prayed against for months —the funeral of my spouse.

As I write these words, my heart is full of gratitude for Bernie's love and life. I am grateful for his illness and for three months spent in a hospital room filled with tender moments of love and grace. I am grateful for the outpouring of support, love and prayer that came forth in the midst of such a profound personal tragedy. And I am grateful to God for his faithfulness, and for the reality that he continually seeks after us, wooing us with opportunities to know and embrace his Fatherly love. In the end, that was what this journey was all about—for Bernie and for me.

Thank you for your love and for carrying Bernie on the wings of prayer into the arms of Our Lord. I am eternally grateful, and I know he is too.

With love and thanksgiving.

Judy

Postscript

Kara's Eulogy to her Dad

Ever since we were children, my father had a favorite question. He would always ask us, "Did anyone ever tell you you're beautiful?" Today, I want to ask him the same question. If I could tell my father one thing, it would be this: "You are a beautiful man, Dad, a beautiful dreamer; and we are so proud of the hero you chose to become."

So many people knew and loved what my family and I have affectionately coined as "the old Bernie"—that aggressive, hilarious businessman who was a cross between Robert De Niro and Jack Nicholson. The old Bernie taught us children many valuable lessons, such as: "Luck is when preparation meets opportunity," and "Packaging is everything."

He would do anything to make people laugh—especially his loved ones—and he never said no to anyone who needed help. Once, while on vacation, he even gave mouth-to-mouth to a little dying bird after we had all just seen the film *Dr. DoLittle*. Bernie Klein had many special gifts, and he knew how to call forth others' gifts as well.

My dad had one desire in life—to take care of his family and to help other people. As long as he was doing that, he felt he was accomplishing his mission in life. But he didn't just serve—he served large; he didn't just dream—he dreamed big. He was a beautiful dreamer, never satisfied with mediocrity, but rather living with enthusiasm to spare.

My dad always told me that when his father died, the priest said at the funeral of Henry Klein Senior, "the church came to him." My father had a similar experience at the end of his life. Not only did the church come to him as he was anointed in the hospital fourteen times, but Christ came to him. My dad became a new man with a new vision, a new heart, and a new life. He was made a new creation in Jesus Christ. Being the man that he was, he still dreamed big about what was to come—about the adventure God had in store for him ahead. I know he is living that adventure today.

Lastly, as I witnessed my father being purified day in and day out, until he took his last breath, I'm grateful to have witnessed the profound love between him and my mother. Truly, they kept their vows till the end, loving each other until "death did they part." My father's last words to my mother were, "I have loved you since the day I met you, and you have always been a jewel in my heart."

Thank you, Daddy, for loving us with all your strength until the end, for giving us a beautiful home and family, for teaching us how to laugh, to live, to love and to dream as you did, Beautiful Dreamer. We will love you forever.

Henry Klein's Eulogy to his brother Bernard

On May 25, 1945, something happened which will never be replicated. Jose Bernardo Gerardo Klein was born into this world, bringing with him more energy and enthusiasm than anyone I've ever known. Bernie was a family man, an entrepreneur, a visionary, a friend, a father and a gentleman. There was no mountain too high to climb, nor any problem too difficult to solve. When people would ask: What does Bernie do? I had a hard time answering. He helped people in trouble. He created opportunities from thin air. His imagination was without bounds; his work ethic was unequaled. His heart was immense and his arms were always open. Bernie Klein lived a full and fulfilling life, never without a smile. When he was very young, he became a United States Marine and was honored for his excellence. After he served his country, he worked for the City of Los Angeles and climbed ladders that weren't even there. Soon thereafter, he became an international strategist for Atlantic Richfield and traveled the globe. When the World's Fair came to New Orleans, he couldn't help himself or curb his imagination. He formed an advertising and communications company and won multiple awards and accolades. But his biggest fight was not to be won on this earth. He received the last rites fourteen times and kept on coming back. He gave us hope against all hope and kept us praying for a miracle. In the end, he died in peace and will be sorely missed by anyone who knew him.

Bernard Joseph Klein, Rest In Peace

Epilogue

After living for over a year in both Florida and Italy in "Communita Cenacolo"—a lay Catholic community with sixty five houses around the world—Kara moved home to New Orleans where she teaches voice and piano lessons to children. She is traveling again giving concerts and chastity talks to teens and just released a new CD of original music, which can be found at www.karaklein.com. Her desire is to minister God's healing power to the lost and brokenhearted though the gifts of word and song.

Alex obtained a Master's Degree in Social Work in December 2012. As part of her educational experience, she did an internship working with victims of domestic abuse and violence and also worked at a local hospital that specializes in eating disorders. She recently moved to New York, where she works at homeless shelter for mentally ill women. She plans to dedicate her life to working with people in recovery from trauma.

Gaby and Grayson were married on November 28, 2009. When they called that night to check on James, they reported that their wedding day was the "best day of their lives." They welcomed another son, John-Henry Bernard, on August 15, 2011, the Feast of the Assumption. He is the spitting image of his aunt Alex and always has a smile on his chubby little face. Their third baby boy, Joseph Francis, was born twenty-one months after John-Henry on May 9, 2013, the Feast of the Ascension.

Christian followed Kara to Communita Cenacolo, entering on June 9, 2010. After living in Italy for a year with twelve of his "brothers" in a convent that houses a dozen nuns, he moved to Austria and Medjugorje before being transferred back to Alabama, where he now lives. He is fluent in Italian and proficient in leading praise and worship for the Community. He reports that he is "at peace" and that he is learning to take life on its own terms.

Benjamin, who is in eighth grade, found an ardent admirer and best buddy in his little nephew James. James' face lights up when he sees his beloved "Unka," reminding us all of what it means to be "well loved" as the circle goes around again. "Unka" loves to make James laugh hysterically, and we never tire of watching their antics. When he's not making James laugh, Benjamin is still playing in the street with his little posse of friends.

As for me, I spend my days quietly: praying, reading, writing and practicing what I like to call "sobriety from chaos." Two years after Bernie's death, I met a Christian counselor and former missionary in the Adoration Chapel of Our Lady of the Lake Church. Mark and I were married on September 29, 2012, the Feast of the Archangels. For our first anniversary, we travelled to Rome to have our marriage personally blessed by Pope Francis. We are constantly in awe of God's mercy and His mysterious ways, as we enjoy the unexpected and delightful gift of being newlyweds.

Acknowledgements

Thank you Heather King for editing *Miracle Man*. Your excellent help and guidance not only filled in the missing gaps in my original manuscript; it challenged me to look more deeply into my own heart. You have inspired me to write—and to keep writing.

Thank you to the many family members and friends who kindly read the manuscript and encouraged me to publish it. Thanks also for giving me invaluable feedback on how to improve it: Carol Gelderman, Cecil Beatrous, Musheer Robinson, Lisa Klein, Hedy Boelte, Mary Lou McCall, Jane Harvey, Phyllis Landrieu, Renee Landrieu, Jessica Nehrbass, Sue Zaunbrecher, Gerard Braud, Sandy Avanzino, Kitty Cleveland, Melanie Arnold, Suzy Neal, Greg Landrieu, Susan Dane, Jessica Goodrum, Pat Hyland, Elizabeth Braud, Annie Boelte Heard and Jimmy Seghers.

Thank you Mom and Dad, for giving me the gifts of life, love, faith, and a Catholic education, for which I am extremely grateful. Thanks especially to you, Mom, for instilling in me, through your example, a love of the written word.

Thank you "Miracle Man," Bernie Klein, who told me many times that my "real vocation" is to be a writer. Thank you for your love, for our family, for our journey together and for giving me such an incredible and inspirational story to write. Requiescat in pace.

Thank you Mark Gelis, my husband, best friend and soul mate. Your friendship, love and kindness have healed me in profound and life-changing ways. Ti adoro!

And thanks be to God—the Father, Son and Holy Spirit—for constantly surprising me with Your tender mercy, love, and goodness. Thank you for giving me so much more than I could ask for or imagine!

Judy Landrieu Klein

Judy Landrieu Klein is a Catholic theologian who speaks a word of holy hope through a dynamic ministry that includes teaching, writing and public speaking. A "revert" to Catholicism, Judy received a Master's Degree in Theological Studies from the University of Dallas in the Jubilee Year 2000. She has also carried out post-graduate doctoral studies in Bioethics at the Regina Apostolorum Pontifical Athanaeum in Rome. Judy served as an adjunct professor of Theology at Our Lady of Holy Cross College in New Orleans for seven years, teaching "Morality and Science" and "Catholic Sexual Ethics." She received the *mandatum* from Archbishop Alfred Hughes in 2004.

Judy is a published author whose books include: *Mary's Way: The Power of Entrusting Your Child To God, Living Water: Understanding The Gift Of New Life Through Baptism* and *Sez Who: Why Church Authority Established By Christ Is So Important To Us Today.*

Judy served as co-host of Radio Maria's *Apologetics Live* program for 4 1/2 years. Additionally, she has appeared on television on EWTN's *Women of Grace* show and Focus Worldwide Television's *Focus* program. She has been the featured speaker at many faith-based events, including *Magnificat* Women's Breakfasts, *Legatus* dinners, and *Theology on Tap* meetings. Most recently, she was a keynote speaker at the *Catholic Women In Action* Advent Day of Reflection, the St. Louis Marian Conference and the Fullness of Truth Conference. Information about her speaking engagements can be found on her website at memorareministries.com.

Judy is the founder of *Memorare Ministries*, which is dedicated to bringing a message of hope and encouragement to those who are suffering. She is married to Dr. Mark Gelis and has seven wonderful children and five beautiful grandchildren. Judy's blog, *Holy Hope*, can be found at memorareministries.com. She also blogs at Aleteia, CatholicMom.com and for the Catholic Writers Guild.